IMAGES
of America

EARLY
HAYWARD

IMAGES
of America

EARLY
HAYWARD

Robert Phelps and
the Hayward Area Historical Society

ARCADIA
PUBLISHING

Copyright © 2004 by Robert Phelps and the Hayward Area Historical Society
ISBN 978-1-5316-1577-2

Published by Arcadia Publishing
Charleston, South Carolina

Library of Congress Catalog Card Number: 2004111036

For all general information contact Arcadia Publishing at:
Telephone 843-853-2070
Fax 843-853-0044
E-mail sales@arcadiapublishing.com
For customer service and orders:
Toll-Free 1-888-313-2665

Visit us on the Internet at www.arcadiapublishing.com

CONTENTS

ACKNOWLEDGMENTS

As a Southern California native who came to the Bay Area seven years ago, writing this book has been truly educational, made possible by the help and insight of several dedicated individuals and institutions.

The Hayward Area Historical Society was indispensable, granting me unfettered access to their superb photographic collections. Jim DeMersman, executive director, supplied the initial enthusiasm for the project; Beth Hansen, collections manager, offered in-depth knowledge of museum collections as well as long hours in front of the photo scanner; and Adrienne McGraw, museum director of education, provided the insight of a born educator and cherished friend.

To interpret the photos, I drew on the combined wisdom of Hayward's past historians, notably John Sandoval, Harwood Hall, and the collective "Eden Writers," to name just a few. Frank Goulart provided many interesting stories of early Hayward, while Banning Fenton reviewed captions and took me on an unforgettable tour of the city's downtown.

Beyond the collected experts in Hayward's local history, my colleagues at the Department of History at California State University, Hayward, have always been there to offer me advice and professional support. Dee Andrews, Hank Reichman, Judith Stanley, Gerald Henig, Pablo Arreola, and Richard Orsi have been exceptional mentors, while Nancy Thompson and Jessica Weiss offered the perspectives of professional peers and valued friends.

Away from the centers of academia, my mother, Gloria, has taught me to meet life's challenges with the mixture of strength and tenderness typical of Kumeyaay women, a lesson I hope never to forget. Special thanks also to my wife Meri. This exceptional woman has long met my physical and mental absences with constant love and encouragement, a gift I know I can never fully repay.

Finally, I would like to dedicate this book to the memory of my father, Woodrow G. Phelps. A veteran of the United States Navy and a member of what Tom Brokaw calls "The Greatest Generation," it was from my father that I gained an unbridled passion for history and the inspiration to pursue life's dreams.

INTRODUCTION

Little did William Hayward, a luckless 49er with a talent for shoe-making, realize when he squatted on land in the Palomares Canyon in 1851 that he committed the first act in the creation of one of the Bay Area's most vibrant communities. First believing that the canyon was federal land, Hayward was convinced otherwise by Guillermo Castro, a former don who had been granted 27,000 acres around San Lorenzo Creek by Mexican governor Juan Baptista Alvarado 11 years earlier. Although the United States acquired California in 1848, the Treaty of Guadalupe Hidalgo stipulated that Mexican land grants be respected; and Castro's mammoth Rancho San Lorenzo Alta included modern-day Hayward, Castro Valley, southern San Leandro, and much to William Hayward's discomfort, the Palomares Canyon.

Impressed by a pair of boots apparently made for him by Hayward, Castro allowed the American to remain, provided he relocate to the flatlands near Castro's adobe home. Hayward complied and opened a small store and hotel on what today is the corner of Main and A Streets, catering to immigrants unwilling to journey to Oakland to purchase supplies. Hayward's Hotel and the city that developed around it were on their way to becoming a major regional crossroads.

Rightly termed the "Heart of the Bay," the city of Hayward owes its existence to geography. The narrow plain between the Walpert Ridge and San Francisco Bay where William Hayward built his hotel was also near the convergence point for the eight tributaries forming San Lorenzo Creek, a sizeable channel that flowed through Castro Valley before its waters dispersed in the marshes bordering the bay. Not only did the creek provide an important water source, but the canyons carved by the tributaries also served as pathways for travel, making the region a natural communications hub between San Francisco, Oakland, and the rich fields of the Livermore Valley.

The advantages of Hayward's natural environment were long recognized by the Ohlone, hunter-gatherers who dwelled in small villages scattered throughout the East Bay. Living on plants and game inhabiting the region, the Ohlone clustered their tule homes on high ground and engaged in regular controlled burns of undergrowth to facilitate gathering activities and encourage the growth of plants sought by game animals.

Spain's defeat in the Seven Years War as well as fears of a Russian incursion into Mexico's northern frontier prompted the Spaniards to occupy Alta California in 1769, changing the lives of the Ohlone and other coastal tribes forever. Father Junipero Serra's Sacred Expedition began in May of that year with the establishment of Mission San Diego. By 1821, Spain established 20 missions along the California coast, charged with converting the region's natives to Roman Catholicism and establishing a loyal population to serve as a bulwark against foreign intrusion.

One of those missions was Mission San Jose de Guadalupe, founded in 1797 to pacify the natives along the southern extremities of San Francisco Bay and protected by the presidio built at its entrance in 1776. To supplement native conversions, the Spaniards also established the pueblo of San Jose on the southern end of the bay and, more importantly for the history of modern Hayward, began the practice of enticing settlement by granting large tracts of land to Spanish colonists.

However, by the end of Spanish rule in Alta California in 1821, the only land grant in the East Bay was that of Luis Peralta, a 45,000-acre tract on the site of modern Oakland. Yet the new Republic of Mexico continued the practice of encouraging colonization through the granting of homesteads. Not only did Guillermo Castro gain Rancho San Lorenzo, but Francisco Soto was awarded a sizeable grant west of modern Hayward's railroad tracks. Employing converted Indians as *vaqueros*, the Castro and Soto families, like the other Californios of the region, made their living as ranchers, tending to vast herds of cattle that they sold overseas in the form of hides, dried beef, and tallow.

Everything changed with the discovery of gold at Sutter's Mill on January 28, 1848. The Gold Rush brought hundreds of thousands of fortune-seekers to the Bay Area, from transient miners on their way to the Sierra foothills to permanent settlers hoping to capitalize on the miners' lack of success in the gold fields. Guillermo Castro saw the possibilities as well and in 1854 laid out the town of San Lorenzo. But in 1864 Castro left for South America, his lands beset by squatters, taxes, and legal fees, and his cattle herds depleted by mismanagement and his own penchant for gambling.

The disintegration of the Rancho San Lorenzo Alta and the surrounding ranchos signaled the advent of a new era for the region. Like other Californios in the Bay Area, the Castros and Sotos met increasing debt by the piecemeal sale of their lands, opening the region to private investors unfettered by the designs of a single individual. Merchants and farmers, attracted by the fertility generated by San Lorenzo Creek and the pathways its tributaries provided, soon occupied the region's canyons and flatlands.

Throughout the Gold Rush era, stagecoaches ran from Hayward to Stockton and the southern gold fields beyond, and by 1865, the San Francisco, Alameda, & Haywards narrow gauge railroad linked the community with San Francisco. More settlers poured in to take advantage of the region's rich soils and transportation links, and in 1876 the town of "Haywards" was incorporated, beginning an era of urbanization and immigration that continues to this day.

Today the city of Hayward encompasses 61 square miles and boasts a population of over 140,000. And still, the city's geography—25 miles southeast of San Francisco, 14 miles south of Oakland, 26 miles north of San Jose, 10 miles west of the Livermore Valley—continues to guarantee its status as a principal regional crossroads. Crisscrossed by multiple federal and state highways and home to a major university, the modern city built by the San Lorenzo Creek is today a diverse, vibrant community that has justly earned the title the "Heart of the Bay."

One

FOUNDATIONS
PRE-CONTACT TO 1868

The Ohlone, the original human inhabitants of the East Bay, were hunter-gatherers who utilized the resources provided by the rich natural environment of the region. Their social structure was centered on small "tribelets" of approximately 250 people. Ohlone men hunted and fashioned tools, boats, and weapons, while women gathered food, wove baskets, and tended to children. Approximately 40 native villages surrounded the bay prior to European contact, and the Yrgin tribelet of the Ohlone inhabited the region that now encompasses modern Hayward.

The arrival of the Spaniards in Alta California changed the lives of the Ohlone forever. Many of the Yrgin were "brought to" Mission San Jose between 1799 and 1805, their former lands incorporated into the mission or distributed among families of Spanish or mixed heritage. By 1840 the area around San Lorenzo Creek was part of the new Republic of Mexico and administered by Guillermo Castro.

In spite of Castro's failure and eventual exile to South America, the influx of Americans taking advantage of the rich agricultural lands and the natural byways of the area meant that the region around William Hayward's hotel was certain to grow. Numerous inns were established on the roads that joined Oakland, San Jose, and the Livermore Valley, and large farms soon dotted the region. In spite of a disastrous earthquake that ravaged much of the region in 1868, the community called "Haywards" was definitely on its way to becoming the "Heart of the Bay."

HAYWARD'S ORIGINAL HUMAN INHABITANTS. In this drawing by Michael Harney, an Ohlone man prepares his boat made of tule rushes. Yrgin villages may have existed at Diramaderos Springs, near San Lorenzo and Holy Sepulcher Cemeteries, and downtown Hayward near the Civic Center. (Illustration courtesy of Malcolm Margolin's *The Ohlone Way*, Heyday Books.)

FIRST CONTACT. In another drawing by Michael Harney, Ohlone women converse while tending to their tasks. First contact between East Bay natives and Europeans occurred during Lt. Pedro Fages's 1772 exploration and Capt. Juan Bautista de Anza's expedition in 1776. Over time, many Yrgin were brought into Mission San Jose. (Illustration courtesy of Malcolm Margolin's *The Ohlone Way*, Heyday Books.)

10

GUILLERMO CASTRO. Castro was born in 1810 on the Rancho de Las Lagas, 10 miles south of the pueblo of San Jose. His father, Joaquin Isidro Castro, arrived in California with Juan de Anza's expedition in 1774. As a young man, Guillermo Castro became an officer in the Mexican Army, served as a lieutenant in San Jose's militia company, and later became the pueblo's surveyor. In 1829, Castro married Maria Luisa Peralta, daughter of the owner of Rancho San Antonio, in present-day Oakland. The couple eventually had seven children, four boys and three girls. The Castro family originally moved to the Hayward area in 1839, building their adobe home near the present location of Hayward's old city hall. Castro chose the site for three reasons: he could water his extensive cattle herd on the San Lorenzo Creek; the area was linked to other Mexican Ranchos by El Camino Real, Spain's old royal highway; and, finally, the land was adjacent to the Peralta grant. The Mexican government granted Castro full legal title to the Rancho San Lorenzo Alta in 1840.

11

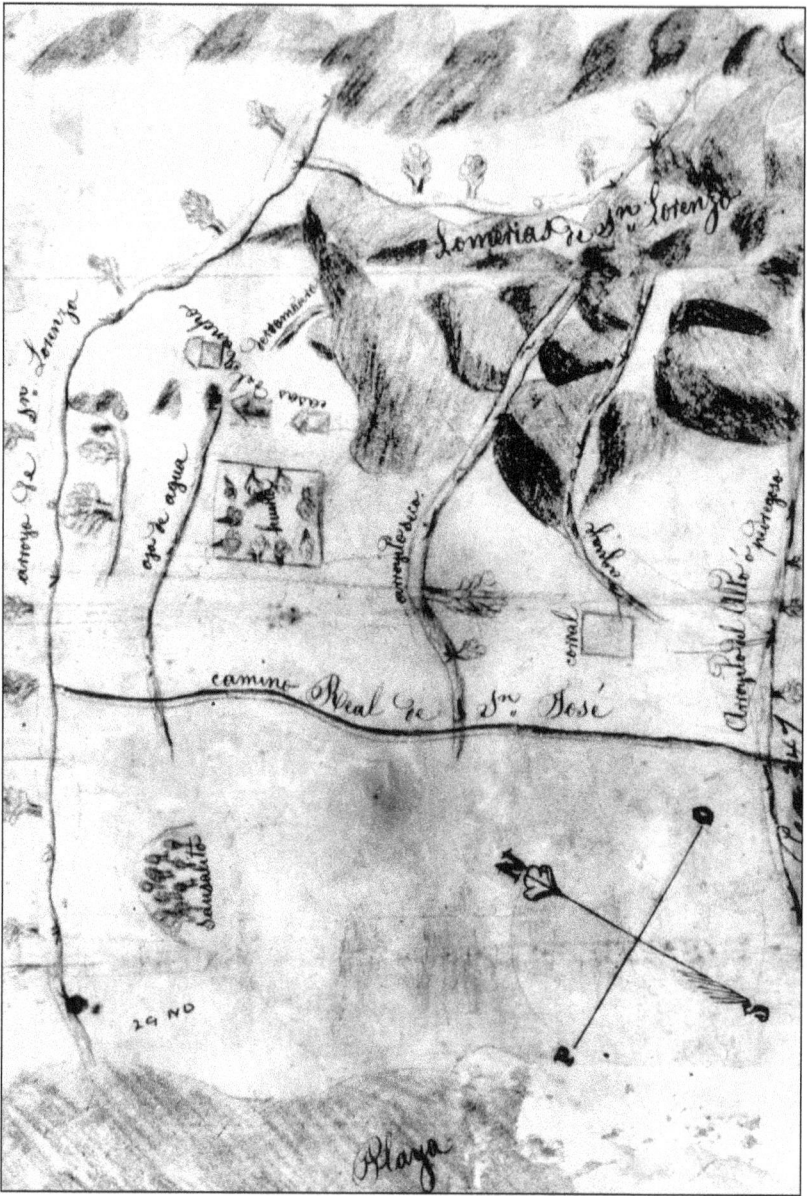

Diseño of Rancho San Lorenzo. Diseños showed the boundaries of Mexican land grants. Castro's grant was approximately 27,000 acres, roughly bordered on the west by what are now the Union Pacific railroad tracks, to the south by the modern axis of Harder Road, and to the east by the East Bay hills. The strip between the Castro grant and San Francisco Bay was awarded to Francisco Soto, who christened his 6,688 acres the Rancho San Lorenzo Baja. Castro's diseño shows, at the drawing's edge, San Lorenzo Creek, while El Camino Real runs across the map's center. After the American conquest, Congress passed the Land Act of 1851 to confirm the title of the Mexican grants. Many Californios were forced to sell much of their holdings to pay attorney fees as their claims moved through American courts. Castro was further crippled by a disastrous trip to Southern California where he lost $35,000 earmarked for the purchase of cattle in a night of gambling. Burdened by numerous debts, Castro gradually sold off his holdings, leaving for South America in 1864.

THE CASTRO ADOBE. The Castro family home was built on a knoll where Hayward's old city hall now stands, between B and C Streets on Mission Boulevard. Below the adobe was a large plaza with corrals and rodeo grounds where *mantanzas*, the seasonal slaughtering of cattle for their hides, meat, and tallow, were carried out. Smaller structures situated around the main adobe housed rancho *vaqueros*, servants, and their families.

ORIOLE, C. 1890. After Castro's departure in the 1860s, his *vaqueros* dispersed throughout the region, probably gaining employment with American ranchers. A Mexican Indian, Oriole was known as one of the last *vaqueros* of the Rancho San Lorenzo, living in a small house near the former Plaza.

13

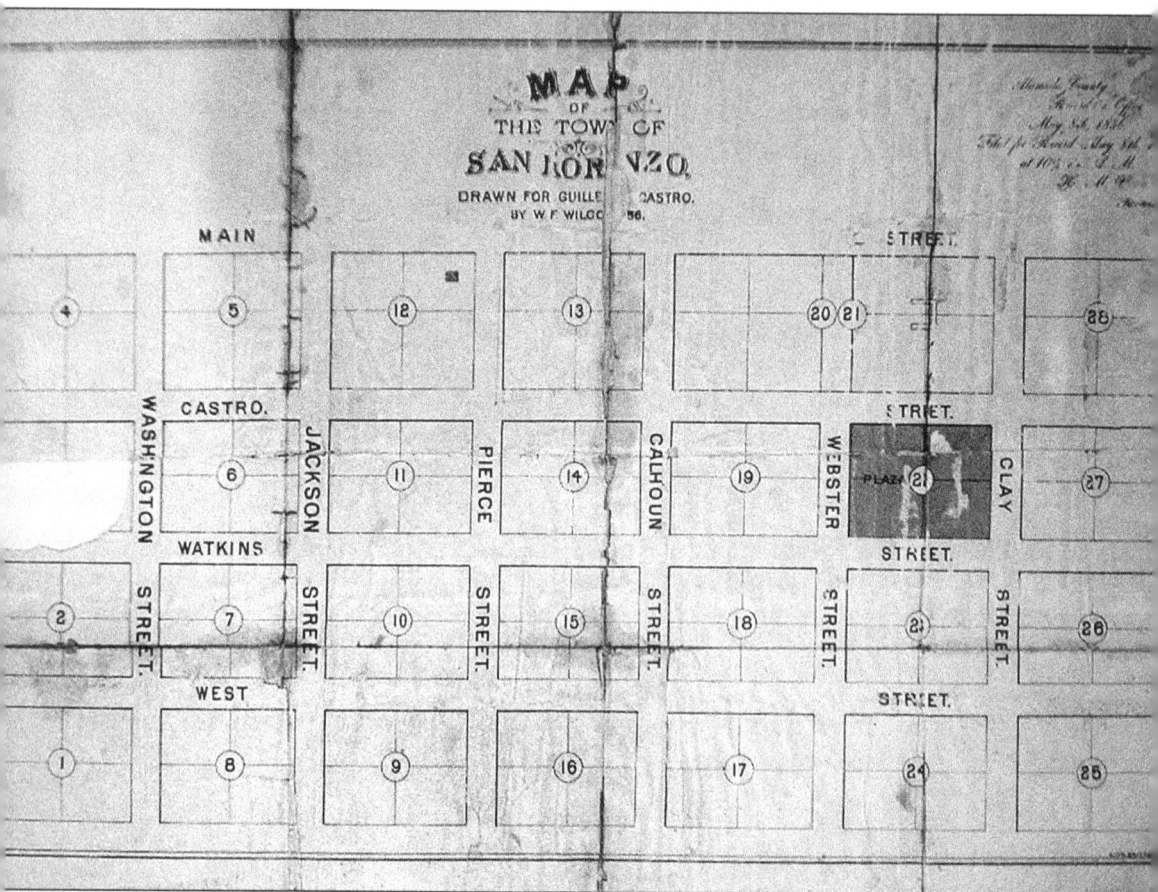

MAP
OF
THE TOWN OF
SAN LORENZO.
DRAWN FOR GUILLE   CASTRO.
BY W. F. WILCO   56.

SURVEY OF THE TOWN OF SAN LORENZO, 1856. Castro attempted to adapt to changing circumstances by subdividing the lots around his adobe and selling them to American settlers then streaming into the East Bay. Castro Street became the main north-south axis of the proposed town of San Lorenzo, while east-west streets were initially named after U.S. presidents. Unfortunately for Castro, his real estate ventures could not save the family fortune, and he was forced to sell much of his holdings to financier Faxon D. Atherton, who renamed the "presidential" streets to the lettered monikers typical of American cities. When William Hayward was appointed postmaster in 1856, residents around the hotel asked the federal government to rename San Lorenzo "Hayward." Because postal regulations prohibited naming a post office after a living person, the U.S. Postal Department adopted the suggestion of Faxon D. Atherton and changed the name of the post office to "Haywood." When the town was incorporated in 1876, the solution was to call the town "Haywards," the removal of the apostrophe circumventing the troublesome regulations.

14

WILLIAM HAYWARD. Hayward was a failed 49er when he arrived in Palomares Canyon in 1851 and made his fortune by catering to travelers between San Francisco and the gold fields. In addition to his role as hotel proprietor and postmaster, Hayward served as an Alameda County road commissioner, a position that allowed him to oversee the development of an extensive road network around the hotel. He died in 1891 at the age of 76.

HAYWARD'S HOTEL, 1876. Development of the 100-room hotel began in 1851, with William Hayward's purchase of property from Guillermo Castro on what is now, approximately, the parking lot of the Comet Auto Supply store on A and Main. At right center is one of the stagecoaches that made regular runs between Hayward's and surrounding East Bay communities. To the far right, dressed in white aprons, are Chinese members of the hotel staff.

ANOTHER VIEW OF HAYWARD'S, C. 1870. Taking advantage of its proximity to nearby mountain passes and William Hayward's position as county road commissioner, the hotel served as a stop for travelers journeying between Oakland and San Jose or to the Livermore and Central Valleys. By 1880, Hayward was also known as a rural resort for San Franciscans eager to get away from the bustle of the city.

COACHES IN FRONT OF HAYWARD'S HOTEL, C. 1870. The constant comings and goings of coaches and buggies at Hayward's underscored the hotel's role as a regional way station, and William Hayward himself operated a stagecoach company. The city's modern crisscrossing by Interstates 880, 580, and State Routes 92, 185, and 238 demonstrate the continued importance of Hayward as a major transportation nexus.

16

OAKES/VILLA HOTEL. Once Hayward's was established as an important destination for East Bay travelers, other hotels followed. Tony Oakes built the Oakes Hotel on Castro Blvd, near B Street. Oakes Hall was built next to the hotel to accommodate various events, including circuses, until an escaped lion dampened the town's enthusiasm. The hotel was located on what is now the parking lot of the Albertson's Store on Mission Boulevard.

CENTRAL HOTEL, C. 1880. Another Hayward's way station, the Central Hotel was located on the corner of Castro and A Streets. Although Hayward's hotel was located on A and Main, most other inns were located on Castro Street (Mission Boulevard), which also served as the main route to San Jose. To the north, the road followed the course of modern East 14th Street, linking Hayward's to Oakland.

WILLIAM MEEK, C. 1900. As Hayward's Hotel became an important crossroads, the surrounding region also developed into an equally important agricultural center. William Meek was one of the first pioneers of commercial agriculture in Alameda County, arriving in Eden Township in 1859. Meek also helped develop Royal Ann and Bing cherries and served as a county supervisor.

MEEK ESTATE. By 1869 Meek had acquired some 3,000 acres, most of which formerly belonged to Soto's Rancho San Lorenzo Baja. Meek's estate included all of the land from what is now Mission Boulevard to Hesperian Boulevard, just past Winton Avenue, and became known as "Cherryland" because of the cherry groves Meek planted. The Hayward Area Historical Society is now restoring the Meek House for use as a museum.

MCCONAGHY HOUSE. Born in Scotland, Neal McConaghy immigrated to the United States in 1848 and arrived in San Lorenzo in 1853. In 1865, McConaghy and his wife, Sarah, purchased 197 acres of farmland along San Lorenzo Creek and began growing wheat and vegetables. In 1886 the couple moved into their new 12-room home along Hesperian Boulevard, then called Telegraph Road.

JOHN MCCONAGHY, 1905. When Neal died in 1914, his son, John, became manager of the McConaghy holdings. Living most of his life in the home built by his parents, John McConaghy died in 1972 at the age of 100. Here he poses with his prize team of carriage horses, Ina and Blossom, in front of Hayward's Hotel.

MCCONAGHY HOUSE TODAY. John McConaghy was 15 years old when he moved into the home constructed for his parents by local builder John Haar Sr. After marrying Florence Smyth in 1903, the couple moved into the McConaghy home to help care for John's ailing parents, who died in 1912 and 1914. When John himself died in 1972, he had lived in the house for 86 years. Today the Hayward Area Recreation District owns the McConaghy House and the Hayward Historical Society maintains it as a museum. Located next to Kennedy Park on Hesperian Boulevard, the preserved estate includes the 12-room house, complete with 1880s-era furnishings, a tank house, and a carriage house. The McConaghy home is decorated for various holiday seasons and is the site of an annual antique show.

LEWELLING FARM. Henderson Lewelling came to California during the Gold Rush with William Meek. After failing as a miner, Lewelling purchased 120 acres from the Soto Estate in what is now the Ashland District of Alameda County on the corner of Hampton Road and East 14th Street. A friend of the Meek family, Lewelling lost his home to the urban development north of San Lorenzo Creek.

SAN FRANCISCO AND ALAMEDA RAILROAD LOCOMOTIVE, J.G. KELLOGG. In early 1865, A.A. Cohen and Faxon D. Atherton reincorporated the San Francisco and Alameda Railroad into the San Francisco, Alameda, & Haywards Railroad. By August the first steam trains rolled into the new Hayward Station, south of the city plaza on present day Watkins Street. Hayward's position as a regional crossroads, heretofore solely dependent on horse-drawn transport, was finally secured.

DAMAGE FROM THE 1868 EARTHQUAKE. On October 21, 1868, a major rupture on the Hayward fault devastated the East Bay. Numerous homes and businesses in Hayward suffered extensive damage. In the foreground stands Edmundson's warehouse, a local grain storage facility completely destroyed by the quake. The white structure in the distant background at left center is Hayward's Hotel, also moderately damaged.

DESTRUCTION OF THE SFA&H SAN LEANDRO DEPOT. Although many of Hayward's businesses suffered damage from the quake, none faired as badly as the San Francisco, Alameda, & Haywards Railroad. Crippled by the financial losses resulting from the disaster, the directors of the SFA&H sold the line to the Central Pacific Railroad. Trains were soon running once again.

Two

THE CHANGING
LANDSCAPE
1868–1900

The natural byways in part formed by San Lorenzo Creek meant that the devastating earthquake of 1868 would only prove a temporary impediment to the development of the area around Hayward's Hotel. Within the year, the Central Pacific Railroad reestablished railroad service to the community, stagecoach operations expanded, and the landscape of the flatlands between the hills and the bay began to change. Although farming was the primary occupation of most area residents, new businesses appeared to serve those involved in agriculture, lodging, and transportation. In short, "Haywards" was undergoing the initial stages of urbanization.

The old route of Spain's El Camino Real, in 1870 known as Castro Street and today called Mission Boulevard, became dotted with shops, blacksmiths, breweries, and livery stables, all supporting the inns serving travelers headed towards Oakland, San Jose, and the Livermore Valley or supplying the farms feeding the region's growing population. Faxon D. Atherton, who purchased a significant portion of Rancho San Lorenzo Alta, subdivided, sold, or donated Castro's former holdings. Atherton's clients developed their lands, graded roads, and built houses and businesses.

New innovations spurred the alteration of Haywards' landscape. Not only the railroad, but the advent of the horsecar and electric streetcar also channeled development in directions recognizable today. B Street became a center of community life, the old Victorian homes that today emanate from downtown testifying to this period of city history. No longer a simple road junction, Haywards was now a town.

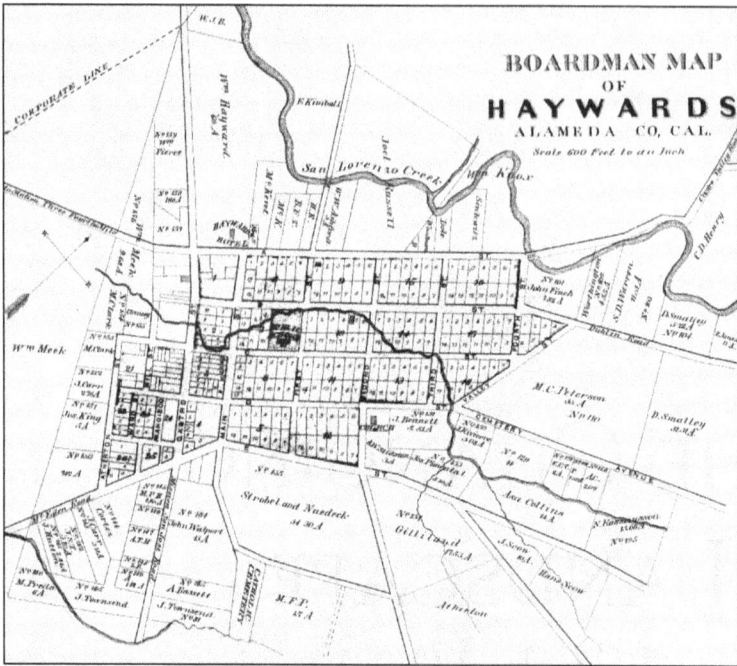

BOARDMAN MAP OF HAYWARDS. This c. 1880 map shows the general outlines of the town. San Lorenzo Creek is clearly visible to the north. Hayward's Hotel appears on the corner of A and Main Streets. The unincorporated village of San Lorenzo, often called "Squattersville" because of the large number of Americans who illegally settled in the area before 1860, was north of the creek.

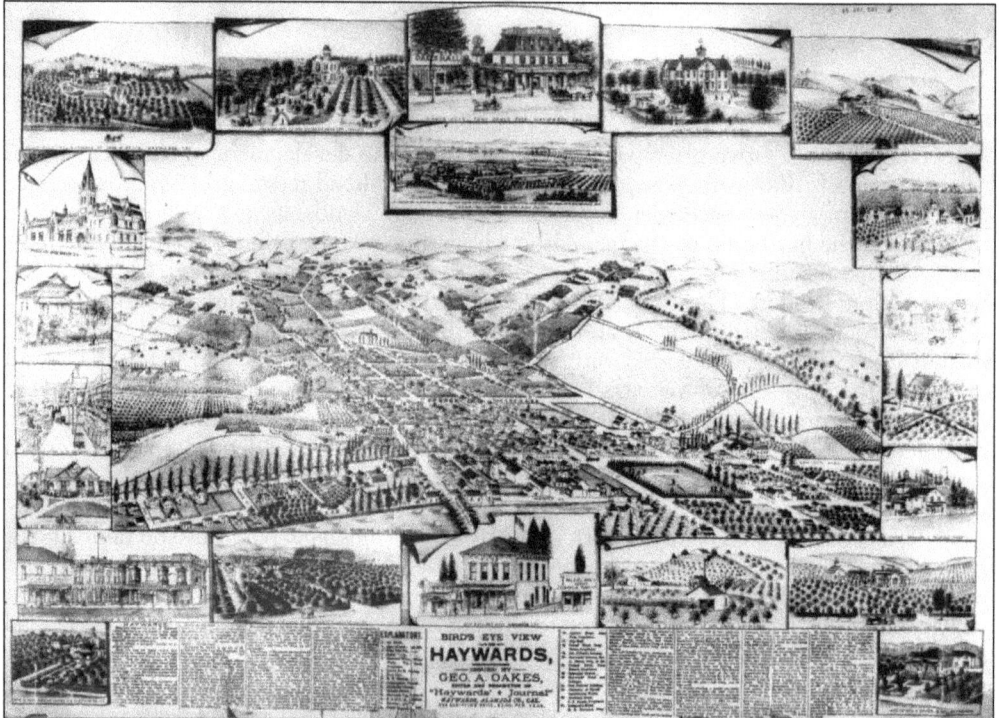

BIRD'S-EYE VIEW OF HAYWARDS, 1889. Appearing in the *Hayward Journal*, George Oakes issued this illustration to advertise the advantages of the community. The lower caption opens, "Here you may see the town of Hayward, you may see it as you would if you were a bird, and halting in your rapid flight should poise on every wing and look at the beautiful prospect before you."

THE TOWN OF HAYWARDS, C. 1900. Taken from Hayward's Hotel, looking south, the street to the left is Main Street and the steeple-topped building in the center is the Native Son's Hall on the southeast corner of C and Main Streets. The built-up area to the right stands along Mission Boulevard, then called Castro Street. In the far background is the present location of California State University, Hayward.

HAYWARDS, LOOKING NORTH, C. 1900. This view is from the rear of a line of homes along E Street and shows the town's mixture of urban and rural features. The Native Son's Hall, again, clearly visible in this photo, was the center of Hayward social life from its inception in 1892 until its removal in the 1930s.

25

HORSECAR LINE, C. 1880. One of the most important factors in the changing landscape of Haywards was the horsecar line developed by H.W. Meek in the 1870s. The line ran from the Southern Pacific Railroad depot to Hayward's Hotel, first east along B Street, and then North on Main. As a result, B Street became one of the town's busiest business sections.

OLD HAYWARD HORSECAR, C. 1890. After years of transporting passengers between the railroad station and Hayward's Hotel, this horsecar, which carried approximately 12 people, looks as though it has seen better days.

HAYWARDS LIVERY STABLE, C. 1890. Horsecars from the stable, which stood on the northeast corner of Main and A Streets, operated on the main B Street line, from the center of town to the Southern Pacific station, while a spur line on Main Street took passengers to Hayward's Hotel. A fire in 1897 destroyed the stable.

CASTRO STREET, BETWEEN A AND B STREETS, C. 1890. In this photo of Castro Street, between A and B Streets, P. Wilbert's real estate office appears in the foreground on the right. The Villa Hotel, formerly Tony Oakes' Oakes Hotel, stands to the left, and Hayward's Livery Stable is visible at the end of the street on the right.

27

CASTRO STREET, C. 1880. The block between B and C Streets was one of early Hayward's busiest business areas. In this photo of Castro Street, looking north from C Street, the Hayward Fire Barn stands to the right, topped by a cupola and fire bell. Auctioned off in 1913, the proceeds helped finance the construction of a new firehouse. The winner of the auction dismantled the old fire barn in order to reuse the lumber.

H. HAAS JEWELRY STORE, C. 1885. The Haas family poses with their carriage in front of their store, located on the East Side of Castro (now Mission Boulevard) and directly across the street from the Oakes Hotel. Note the driveway on the right, probably leading to a back lot horse barn. Barns were often converted into automobile garages in the early 20th century.

HAYWARD'S FREE MARKET, C. 1890. The Lamb family operated Hayward's Free Market on the west side of Mission Boulevard, between Jackson and E Streets. The Lambs, who lived above the store, bartered their merchandise for agricultural produce. The boards leaning against the sides of the building were used to cover the front of the store at night.

LYON'S BREWERY, C. 1880. Lyon's Brewery was built in 1857 on Castro Street (now Mission Boulevard). Note the misspelling on the sign, incorrectly identifying the establishment as "Loyn's Brewery." Haywards was home to two breweries, Lyon's and the New York Brewery, the latter established in 1866 by John Booken and Henry Hulm. Locals probably consumed beer produced at these two establishments.

CITY STABLES, C. 1880. Not only did stable owners Geary and Grindell operate this livery on the west side of Castro Street (now Mission Boulevard) between A and B Streets, they also owned one of Hayward's undertaking establishments. The stables were next to Tony Oakes's Villa Hotel; the undertaking business was too.

EGGERT'S BLACKSMITH SHOP, C. 1878. Like all small American towns, Haywards was home to a number of blacksmiths. Built in the late 1860s, J. L. River originally operated Eggert's Blacksmith Shop before Henry Eggert, a former employee, purchased the establishment. In the photo, Eggert stands in the doorway, second from left.

SECOND LYON'S BREWERY, C. 1890.
After a fire destroyed the original Lyon's Brewery, the firm built a new brick and wood structure on E Street, with the brewery front on Castro (now Mission Boulevard). The material used to make the brick for the second structure came from the lot occupied by the brewery. Prohibition eventually forced the brewery to close permanently.

CASTRO STREET, C. 1900. The electric streetcar route, established in 1892, lined Castro Street, north of downtown, with single-family dwellings, making the outer reaches of the road Hayward's first streetcar suburb.

CORNER OF B AND CASTRO STREETS, C. 1890. Traditionally one of the busiest sections of downtown Hayward, this photo shows the dirt roads of the early city. The Schafer Building, home of the Price House, a dry goods retailer, and Ramage Hardware occupy the northeast corner.

THE PARLOR SHOE STORE, C. 1870. Note the billboard mounted on the roof, advertising the wonders of "Hassmer's Lung and Cough Syrup." Pictured here on the northeast corner of B and Main, the 4th man from the right is J.L. River; and Henry Eggert, who walked over from their blacksmith shop to be in the photograph, appears on the extreme right.

B STREET, C. 1890. This view looks southwest toward Castro Street. The horsecar tracks are visible along the center of the street.

B STREET, C. 1900. Looking east towards the edge of town, the absence of horsecar tracks indicates that this is B Street, east of Main, the rails turning north at Main towards Hayward's Hotel.

OPENING DAY. Running for 14.3 miles from Oakland to the Hayward terminus near the present location of the Plunge, the Oakland, San Leandro, and Haywards Electric Railway Company's line was the longest in the nation when it began operations on May 7, 1892. Harry W. Meek, William Meek's son, served as company president. Here, dignitaries celebrate in front of the Oakes Hotel.

PAINTING OF THE OAKES HOTEL. OSL&H Electric Railway cars were a regular sight on Castro Street (now Mission Boulevard). The line stimulated real estate development from the downtown area on a north-south axis. Eventually transportation mogul "Borax" Smith purchased the company, and it was later incorporated into the Bay Area's famous Key System. Artist Lester Kent painted this picture.

OSL&H ELECTRIC RAILWAY CAR NO. 2, 1893. The railway used a number of car types. The Carter Brothers Car Company in Newark, California, built the original six cars. Later, the railway ordered larger convertible cars with removable side panels for warm weather. All OSL&H cars wore a red coat of paint. The first car departed Oakland at 5 a.m.; the last car left at midnight.

ANTI-DUST SYSTEM. Between Oakland and Hayward, OSL&H cars followed the course of the very dusty Hayward County Road (now East Fourteenth Street). To combat passenger discomfort and possible fouling of the machinery, the trolley company devised a water sprinkler tank and attached it to the cars. The small spray thrown down by the tank helped to dampen the dust.

PIGGYBACK OPERATION. In 1896 the line began a "piggyback" operation between Hayward and San Leandro. Dispatching company-owned, horse-drawn wagons to pick up freight, teamsters would unhitch the horses and load the wagons onto flatcars pulled by the trolleys. The freight usually made its way to the port of Oakland for shipping; imports came into the Hayward area using the reverse procedure.

HAYWARD HORSECAR ON PARADE. The Hayward Area Historical Society restored one of the original Hayward horsecars, which is now displayed by the museum for special events. Here, the car, with specially modified wheels, pulls excited passengers during Oakland's 1982 St. Patrick's Day parade.

Three

BUILDING A NEW COMMUNITY
1868–1900

Alameda County was created by an act of the state legislature on March 25, 1853. The county was further subdivided into Contra Costa, Clinton, Washington, Murray, Oakland, and Eden Townships. The last of these included much of the Rancho San Lorenzo, and by 1876, continued growth around San Lorenzo Creek and Hayward's Hotel inspired residents to incorporate the city of "Haywards." Because of a law that prohibited the naming of a post office for a living person, the U.S. Postal Service christened the new town's post office "Haywood," condemning 19th-century letter writers and 20th-century historians to utter and seemingly endless confusion. And, as the town of Haywards found its name and its landscape filled with homes and businesses, the 2,000 souls who lived in the area by 1900 forged a new community.

Alongside businesses and farms, the people of Haywards built their first schools, with graduating classes as large as 12 students. The town's Portuguese community crowded local streets and fields with marches and picnics. As with so many American towns, the Fourth of July saw the largest celebrations. Churches appeared: Eden Congregational, First Methodist, and many others. The *Hayward Review* and the *Hayward Journal* became the town's rival newspapers, the latter's baseball team terrorizing local diamonds with its sterling play. Weddings, birthdays, anniversaries, and family outings broke up the monotony of work and learning. And protecting it all was Hayward's Volunteer Fire Company No. 1, led in part by none other than hotel proprietor William Hayward.

CROWD IN FRONT OF HAYWARD'S HOTEL, C. 1880. Although the town of Haywards grew significantly after the 1868 quake, William Hayward's old hotel remained a focal point of community life. By the 1880s Hayward added a Mission-style facade and colored shingles, and "Hayward's Hill" was partially graded to make way for A Street. The original ground level of the hotel was at the top of the steps shown in this photo. Hayward himself was elected justice of the peace in 1878, held the position of town postmaster for 34 years, and served two terms as supervisor of Eden Township. Married twice and the father of two, Hayward was also a member of the First Methodist Church, the volunteer fire company, and the town guard. By the time of his death in 1891, Hayward's Hotel, along with its guest cottages and furnishings, was appraised at $65,000.

HAYWARD'S VOLUNTEER FIRE COMPANY NO. 1. Posing in front of Hayward's Hotel, the red-shirted Volunteer Fire Company No. 1 included some of the most prominent members of Hayward's early community. Standing from left to right are store owners Alex Allen and H.F. Larabee, hotel proprietor William Hayward, Chris Herman, land manager C.T. Ward, land developer and railroad owner Faxon D. Atherton, Asa Collins, blacksmith J.L. Rivers, farmer A.R. Hall, and Charles Barnes. Behind the company is the town's first fire-fighting apparatus, a "Jeffries" hand pumper purchased in the aftermath of the 1868 earthquake. Operated by 12 men on each side and mounted on a red and gold mahogany cart, the Jeffries pumped 300 gallons a minute and served until replaced by a horse-drawn engine in 1908. The Jeffries is still in existence, though thankfully not in use, at the Hayward Fire Department's fire control station at the corner of C and Main Streets.

HAYWARD REVIEW OFFICE, 1880. A wagon and unidentified driver wait outside the office of the *Hayward Review*. Established in 1891 as the *Republican Review*, the paper began as a weekly until principal owner S.C. Smith increased publication to twice a week. The *Review* did not become a daily newspaper until 1925. From 1915 to 1927, the *Revista Portuguesa*, a Portuguese language newspaper, also served Hayward.

GEORGE OAKES, C. 1880. A fixture in Hayward for decades, George Oakes purchased the *Hayward Journal* in 1882 from newspaperman Frank Dallam. Charles Coolridge founded the *Journal*, Hayward's first weekly paper, five years earlier. Oakes published the *Journal* for over 40 years, his work only ending with his death in the 1920s.

THE JOURNALS OF HAYWARD, JULY 1887. The *Journal* also sponsored a baseball team, with games usually played on a field to the west of Bret Harte School. In the front row, from left to right, are players Powell, Manager George Oakes, and W. Smalley. In the back row, from left to right, are team members Clark, Dyer, G. Smalley, Owens, Cahill, Garcia, Dyer, and Long. Tim Cowles, the team mascot, is seated with the bat.

NATIVE SONS HALL. Located at the corner of C and Main Streets, the meeting center of Haywards' Native Sons and Daughters of the Golden West was built by John D. Haar at a total cost of $35,000. For the first half-century of Hayward history, the Native Sons Hall was arguably the most conspicuous feature of the town's built environment, its tower visible from considerable distances (see the panoramic photos of the town on page 25). Beyond the Native Sons and Daughters, numerous Hayward organizations rented the hall for various social events. Hayward's Presbyterian Church reserved the structure for its initial services, schools held their graduation exercises there, and in 1906 the hall was outfitted to feed over 1,000 homeless San Franciscans in the aftermath of the great earthquake. Native Sons Hall was finally demolished in the 1930s to make way for a supermarket, which the fire control station of the Hayward Fire Department later supplanted. The fire control station still stands directly across Main Street from the Hayward Area Historical Society.

LAUREL GRAMMAR SCHOOL.
Hayward's first grammar
school was the Hughes
School, a small structure that
today serves as a residence
on Third Street. The
Laurel School once stood
on the present site of the
abandoned downtown Lucky
Store, where construction
will soon begin on a new
multiplex theater. The Dania
Society purchased half of
the Laurel School structure,
while the other half of the
building was used for grades
one through four until a fire
destroyed it.

PALOMARES SCHOOL. As the population of the old Eden Township increased, new schools opened. The Palomares Grammar School was built near the site where William Hayward originally squatted on Guillermo Castro's land. Instruction began in 1868 with 34 children from grades one through eight. The bell at the top of the structure became a new addition in 1896.

SAN LORENZO SCHOOLCHILDREN. San Lorenzo Grammar School was built in 1859 and was the first permanent school in San Lorenzo Village. The building served until a larger wood structure replaced it in 1902. Here, San Lorenzo's first and second graders pose for a class photo in 1897. Fire destroyed the second San Lorenzo School in 1928 and a two-story brick structure replaced it the following year.

FIRST UNION HIGH SCHOOL, C. 1900. Hayward Union High School, District No. 3, formed in 1892. A total of 18 students met during the first year on the top floor of the Markham Grammar School, followed by the Native Sons Hall. Construction of Hayward's first high school, shown above, finished in 1894 at a cost of $3,000.

HAYWARD UNION HIGH SCHOOL
GRADUATES. Here, Dr. John Gamble,
principal of Union High, poses with
Hayward's first high school graduating
class in 1895. These students would
have taken their secondary education at
three successive locations: the Markham
School, Native Sons Hall, and Union
High School. By 1910, Union High
accommodated 86 students.

HAYWARD TEACHERS, 1885–1886. These
dedicated Hayward teachers include,
from left to right, (front row) Bessie Craig
Dowd, a "Miss Tucker," and Kate Gilbert;
(back row) Kittie Heath, Lizzie Waterbury,
Frank Porter Smalley, and Lelia Smalley.

WILLIAM HAYWARD JR. Even after William Hayward's death, the Hayward family's prominence continued through his widow, Rachel, and their son, William Hayward Jr. Here, William drives a buggy with lifelong friend Charles D. Long around 1870.

W. OTTO EMERSON. W. Otto Emerson, "Hayward's Artist and Naturalist," lived in his "Palm Cottage" home on Foothill Boulevard from around 1879 until his death in 1940. It was at Palm Cottage that Emerson studied, drew, painted, and photographed Bay Area birds and other subjects. An accomplished ornithologist and skilled taxidermist, the Smithsonian Institution's Department of Ornithology in Washington, D.C., has some of Emerson's specimens in its collection today.

EDEN CONGREGATIONAL CHURCH. In 1867, Eden Congregational Church constructed its permanent building on the southeast corner of A and First Streets, after having met for two years on the second floor of a general store on the corner of B and Main Streets. The Colonial-style church served its congregation until 1947.

FIRST PRESBYTERIAN CHURCH. Hayward's Presbyterian Church began services in 1891 with 22 members. Initial meetings were held at Native Sons Hall, but in 1894 the church built a permanent structure on B Street between First and Second. A manse was added in 1908.

CHURCHES ON B STREET. This photo shows the church steeples of the First Presbyterian and First Methodist Church on B Street. In 1866, real estate developer Faxon D. Atherton donated a lot for Hayward's First Methodist Church of Hayward. Built on the corner of B and Second Streets, the church replaced a number of earlier meeting places used by the congregation, including a former saloon.

AGAPIUS HONCHARENKO. Born in 1832 in the Ukraine and a Greek Orthodox priest, Honcharenko immigrated to the United States after the tsarist government exiled him for protesting the status of peasants in the Russian Empire. In 1865, Honcharenko arrived in Hayward with his wife, Albina, conducting Greek Orthodox services in a cave in the Hayward Hills.

AGAPIUS HONCHARENKO AND ADMIRER, 1914. Honcharenko baptized the children of dozens of Russian immigrants, as well as a few Americans. The author of two books designed to assist Russian immigrants, *The School and Family Russo-American Primer* and *The Russian-English Phrase Book*, Honcharenko, wearing his long coat and Cossack-style hat, occasionally served as a guest speaker at Hayward churches and public meetings.

HONCHARENKO. Honcharenko continued criticizing the tsarist regime after his arrival in California and lived in constant fear of assassination by Russian agents. In Hayward, he lived in a small cottage and earned a living by bartering fruits and vegetables for staples and clothing, which he transported by donkey. He died in 1916 at the age of 84.

HAYWARD PARADE. By the end of the 19th century Hayward was home to numerous parades. Here, an unidentified band marches down a Hayward boulevard, probably Castro Street, around 1890.

IDES PICNIC, 1899. Portuguese Americans have been an important part of Hayward since the 1850s, when Portuguese immigrants from the Azores purchased large tracts of land from Guillermo Castro. These early immigrants paid from $100 to $300 per acre for ranchland, with lots varying from 2 to 160 acres. Here, members of the Portuguese community take part in a picnic after the IDES parade of 1899.

IDES PARADE, 1899.
The Portuguese
Irmandade do Divino
Espirito Santo
(Brotherhood of
the Divine Spirit)
constructed its
headquarters building
on C Street in 1898. In
1899 the group began
its IDES procession in
Hayward. The festival
commemorates the
salvation of the Azores
from famine, a tradition
begun by Queen Isabel
of Portugal in the
13th century. Here the
parade works its way
down Castro Street
(Mission Boulevard).

PARADING FIRE ENGINE. The Hayward Fire Department replaced its handcart with a horse-drawn engine in 1908. Driver John Carr trained the horse team to alert him of incoming calls when he was out. One of the horses would walk over to the ringing phone and wait there until Carr returned. After Hayward converted to a Packard engine, it took Carr longer to start the truck than to hitch his horses.

JAMES HARVEY STROBRIDGE. Strobridge came to California during the Gold Rush and was later employed by the Central Pacific Railroad as superintendent of construction for the western portion of the transcontinental railroad. Strobridge oversaw the breaching of the Sierras with his largely Chinese work crews. In 1869 he decided to settle near Hayward, purchasing 500 acres in Castro Valley and building a house on Redwood Road.

THE STROBRIDGE HOUSE, C. 1890. Around his new home, Strobridge planted apricot and pear orchards and raised cattle. He continued working for the Central Pacific, supervising the construction of track between Niles and Oakland as well as links between other points. When construction of the Castro Valley BART station threatened to destroy the house, a compromise ultimately allowed the Strobridge home to remain near the station parking lot.

TAKING A PICTURE AT THE STROBRIDGE HOUSE. Strobridge was married three times. When Maria Keating Strobridge died in 1891, Strobridge married Kate Moore. When she, too, died in 1895, Strobridge married again, this time to Margaret McLean. A woman preparing her camera while Strobridge family members look on begs the question "who's taking the picture?"

THE STROBRIDGE FAMILY. Strobridge family members frolic before the camera in a rare candid photo for the era. By 1880, the advent of easy-to-use dry-plate glass negatives increased the number of amateur photographers and camera clubs throughout the nation.

53

TWO HAYWARD GIRLS, C. 1890. Adults might engage in horseplay for the camera, but not these two Hayward children, who pose for their formal portrait. Late 19th-century fashion generally dictated that children wear carbon copies of adult clothes.

TWO HAYWARD BOYS, C. 1890. George and Louis Heiser of Hayward make serious subjects for East Bay photographer F.E. Cone in 1899. Painted portraits were always within reach for the wealthy, but in the second half of the 19th century photographic equipment made family and childhood portraits a common pleasure for average Americans.

BRIDAL FASHIONS IN HAYWARD, c. 1890. Middle-class brides also enjoyed posing for their pre-nuptial portraits. Here, Flora Palmtag shows off her wedding dress.

A BRIDESMAID IN HAYWARD, c. 1890. Here, Lean Palmtag, age 18, proudly displays her bridesmaid dress.

THE SILVA FAMILY. The growth of the Portuguese community owed much to the ease of travel brought about by the completion of the transcontinental railroad. During the 1870s, approximately 10 percent of the population of Alameda County was Portuguese. In Hayward, the percentage of the population of Portuguese decent may have been as high as 40 percent. Here, Mrs. P.F. Silva poses with her children Amelia, Manuel Anna, and Clara.

BUD, C. 1900. When Bud was born, the city of Hayward was a quiet community of roughly 2,000 individuals with a vibrant but compact downtown surrounded by fruit orchards and truck gardens; a mixture of urban and rural life that still characterizes the Hayward landscape. Having his portrait taken around 1900, three-year-old Bud wears one of the sailor suits popular with parents during the period.

Four

Into a New Century
1900–1920

As Hayward entered the 20th century, a sense of change was in the air. In 1911 the community officially dropped the "s" in its name, and "Haywards" would forever more be known as "Hayward." The town's founders passed into history, and a new generation guided the community into the 20th century.

Hayward's Ladies Improvement Club convinced Andrew Carnegie to finance the town's first library. Hayward's Union High School, one of the most beautiful schools in California, also added to the community's pride. Danish residents purchased the old Laurel School, moved it across B Street, and created a striking meeting hall. Local Catholics built All Saints Church, a magnificent structure that still stands today.

The population of Hayward rose to 3,487 by 1920, and houses continued to supplant family farms. The Meek orchard was subdivided to make room for more residents, while automobiles replaced the horse-drawn buggies that dominated East Bay roads since the Gold Rush. Yet in spite of its steady growth, much of Hayward's economy continued to center on agriculture. Family farms covered the flatlands and canyons around downtown, and Hunt's Cannery, established in the 1890s, became Hayward's largest employer.

But in spite of the good times, as the second decade of the 20th century wore on, Hayward residents were caught in the web of a wider history. The city's Company H helped secure the California border during the Pancho Villa affair, while other Hayward youths found themselves across the Atlantic serving in America's first global war.

OAKES WEDDING ANNIVERSARY. By 1900, Hayward's founders had entered their golden years, and a new generation waited to carry on their work. Here Tony and Pauline Oakes, at center left, celebrate their 50th wedding anniversary in 1901. Oakes, who came to Hayward in 1863, was the proprietor of the famous Oakes Hotel. To the right of the Oakes is Rachel Hayward, widow of town father William Hayward. Although William garnered much of the credit for the success of the hotel, it was Rachel, who came to California via the Isthmus of Panama in 1851, whose hospitality town residents recalled. In her later years she operated a small hotel in Hayward Park at the present location of the Plunge at Memorial Park on Mission Boulevard. Rachel died in 1913 at the age of 86.

RURAL LIFE IN HAYWARD. In spite of the growth of central Hayward, most of the region retained its rustic character. Just outside the downtown area, the bustle of town life gave way to a rural setting. Here the Holmes family poses for the camera, probably at the home of Agapius Honcharenko.

HORTICULTURE IN HAYWARD. Between 1850 and 1900, grains such as wheat, barley, and oats, were the primary crops harvested in Eden Township. By the 1890s Hayward made the transition from extensive to intensive agriculture, and fruits and vegetables were the mainstay of local farmers. Canneries would soon follow. Here resident Myrtle Tupper tends to her orchard around 1910.

HUNT'S CANNERY, C. 1920. Closer to town, the signs of modern corporate agriculture began to appear. The Hunt brothers, Joseph and Will, moved their fruit and vegetable packing company to Hayward in 1896 in order to be closer to its source of peaches, cherries, and other agricultural delicacies. This photo shows the center of the Hunt's compound, looking south.

HUNT'S CANNERY. Employees work on loading docks crowded with crates on the northwest end of the cannery. Looking west, to the extreme right is Hayward's railroad depot, Hunt's vital link to its national market.

HUNT'S CANNERY, C. 1920. In the company's preparation room, Hunt's workers ready fruit for shipping. For over 75 years Hunt's was Hayward's largest employer, with approximately 1,000 permanent employees and roughly 4,000 seasonal workers.

HUNT'S CANNERY, C. 1915. In this photo, female employees are hard at work cooking fruits and vegetables while stacks of canned fruit and vegetables await shipment. Many Hayward residents can recall the periodic smell of fruit or vinegar floating over the town during canning season.

HAUSCHILDT BUILDING, C. 1900. Within downtown itself, change was in the air. The Hauschildt Building on B Street and Foothill Boulevard housed a bicycle shop and grocery. The Hauschildt family also operated a ranch in the Hayward Hills, purchased by Danish immigrant Tim Hauschildt in the 1860s. The Hauschildt heirs eventually sold the ranch to the state of California, the land becoming the campus of California State University, Hayward.

HAUSCHILDT BUILDING, C. 1930. After 20 years the building still stands, but everything else has changed. The streets are paved, crosswalks are painted, and the building has undergone renovations. A three-story structure stands in a former vacant lot. Modern automobiles have replaced the horse-drawn wagon. One means of identifying extensively renovated buildings is by examining their window patterns, which rarely change.

Last Hors Car. Line Ran From CasrSt to S.P. Depot Hayward

HORSECAR LINE, C. 1890. In the 1890s Meek's horsecar line was acquired by the Oakland, San Leandro, and Haywards Electric Railway Company and became a feeder to the main line running along Castro Street (now Mission Boulevard). Here, the old horse-drawn "Car Number 00," the last horsecar in Alameda County, makes its final run in 1909.

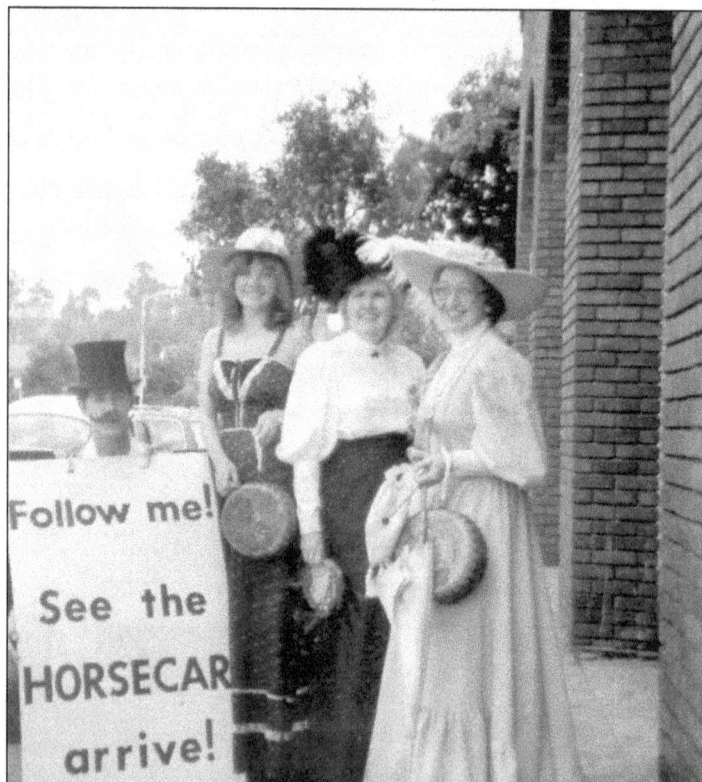

Follow me!

See the

HORSECAR

arrive!

THE HORSECAR REMEMBERED. The Hayward Area Historical Society still maintains the old horsecar (see the photo of its participation in an Oakland parade on page 36) for use in regional celebrations. Here modern horsecar enthusiasts in full costume prepare to greet the car as the HAHS prepares to "reenact a pulling" in 1983.

HAYWARD STREET SCENE, 1910. An early two-seat automobile parks in front of the Kelly Brothers store on B Street. The Bank of Haywards is to the left.

SOUTHERN PACIFIC TRAIN DEPOT, C. 1900. Here an African-American worker, perhaps an employee of the railroad, crosses the Southern Pacific tracks. The Southern Pacific Railroad had long employed African Americans for a variety of jobs. Hayward's black population, like California as a whole, was extremely small until the defense jobs created by World War II spurred the great migration of African Americans to the Pacific Coast.

PRIMARY ELECTION BOARD, 1912. While Hayward's economy continued to grow, the city's women made important strides. In 1912 California women gained the right to vote, and that same year women served for the first time on the Hayward's election board. Here Mrs. A. Kelly and Francis McKeever work with male members of the board on the northeast corner of Main and B Streets.

HAYWARD NURSES. Women weren't just voting; some were actively pursuing careers. Here local nurses pose for the camera around 1910. Before World War II, many working women could be found employed in sales or clerical positions in Hayward's offices and shops. Large firms such as Hunts Brothers relied heavily on local women as their seasonal labor force.

FAIRMONT HOSPITAL. Originally called the Alameda County Public Infirmary when it opened in 1864, Fairmont Hospital was composed of this 36- by 56-foot wooden structure and utilized unheated tents during bed shortages. As the ill were usually cared for at home and visited by doctors making housecalls, many Fairmont "inmates," as they were called, were "indigent ill," as well as elderly patients without family to care for them.

HAYWARD TELEPHONE OPERATORS. Hayward's telephone operators work the switchboards as a female supervisor looks on in this 1908 photo. In 1883 Hood's Drugstore became the first telephone owner in Hayward. By 1897 the Sunset Telephone and Telegraph Company, which operated the town's first centralized service, had 23 subscribers. The town's first telephone exchange was located on B Street.

MARKHAM SCHOOL, 1908. Completed in 1904 on First Street between B and C Streets and originally called Hayward Grammar School, this school was later renamed to honor local poet Edwin C. Markham, who served as principal of Hayward's original grammar school between 1889 and 1890. The Markham School was demolished in 1953 to make way for the downtown Lucky One-Stop Shopping Center.

GRADUATES. Note the distinctive ribbons worn by this group of Hayward graduates in 1910.

ALL SAINTS CHURCH. Roman Catholicism came to the Hayward area with the establishment of Mission San Jose in 1797. During the Mexican era, the padres serving at the mission conducted services for the entire Catholic population of the East Bay in the homes of the leading dons. In Hayward itself, the first Catholic church was established on land donated by Faxon D. Atherton in 1869 on the corner of D and Second Streets. All Saints Parish was created in 1898, and in 1905, Father Viladomat, pastor of All Saints, began planning the construction of a new permanent building. Partially based on the cathedral of his hometown of Berga, Spain, the church exterior was finished in 1909. The interior of the church was not completed until 1923. Renovated in 1980 and substantially repaired in recent years, in 2004 All Saints Church received the Hayward Area Historical Society's Organizational Achievement Award for Historical Preservation.

HAYWARD LIBRARY, 1906. Spurred by the efforts of Hayward's Ladies Improvement Club, in 1905 steel magnate and philanthropist Andrew Carnegie donated $10,000 for the building of the town's first permanent library. It replaced a reading room housed in successive business buildings. Located on the northeast corner of B and First (now Foothill) Streets, the photo, taken in 1906, shows damage caused by the San Francisco earthquake. After the quake, the Hayward's Ladies Improvement Club once again contacted Andrew Carnegie, who donated an additional $1,000 to repair the damage. Although the Carnegie Library survived the quake, it could not survive development along Hayward's business "Strip." The library finally closed on December 31, 1948, its replacement built on Plaza Square and in part financed by the sale of the Carnegie lot. Today the site of the old Carnegie Library is occupied by a mixed-use commercial building.

HAYWARD SCHOOL CHILDREN, C. 1900. Even 100 years ago, Hayward's student body demonstrated a growing diversity.

HAYWARD GRAMMAR SCHOOL CLASS, C. 1920. Teacher Mrs. Gould stands at the far left while proud children pose for their class photo. Like the previous photo, this Hayward Grammar class reflected the growing diversity of the East Bay in the early 20th century.

UNION HIGH SCHOOL. Union High School opened in 1913 on Foothill Boulevard, just north of San Lorenzo Creek. Eventually the grounds included over 40 acres and the school served all eligible students in the old Eden Township. The school won a number of architectural awards.

ARCHITECTURAL CONCEPT OF UNION HIGH SCHOOL. Note the mix of horse, automobile, and streetcar transportation. Although the Union High design won a number of architectural awards and became one of the most recognizable structures in the city, this school and Markham Grammar were demolished in the 1960s to make way for the development of the "Strip" along Foothill Boulevard north of San Lorenzo Creek.

LAUREL SCHOOL MEMORIAL. Here Laurel School faculty and students gather for a memorial service for President William McKinley, who was assassinated in Buffalo in September 1901.

LAUREL SCHOOL, C. 1900. By the early 1900s, the Laurel School was beginning to outlive its usefulness and was slated for replacement. The front portion of the school went up for auction and the Hayward Dania Society acquired it. The man in the hat at the extreme left is poet Edwin Markham.

DANIA SOCIETY. Hayward's Danish community established the Dania Society in the late 1800s. In 1905, the Dania Society paid $200 for the core section of the old Laurel School building and moved it across B Street at a cost of $1,000. The following year, Dania Hall served as an emergency hospital for victims of the great San Francisco earthquake. Today Hayward's Medical Market on Foothill occupies the site.

DANISH LODGE VALBORG. Dania Hall remained the headquarters of Hayward's Thyra No. 9 and Valborg No. 1 lodges until 1952. Here female lodge members ride in a decorated wagon with male escorts during the 1910 Fourth of July parade.

DECORATING A PARADE AUTOMOBILE, C. 1915. Hayward was home to numerous marches and parades, including a Fourth of July Parade, the Portuguese community's annual IDES march, and a bicycle race. Early parades featured participants solely on foot or horseback, but after 1900 increasing numbers of automobiles, decorated with flowers or branches, were used in local celebrations. Here Hayward Union High girls pose before arranging spring blossoms on their Model T.

"SHOTGUN!" The girls board their auto and prepare to move on to participate in the Spring Blossom Festival. It is unclear whether their decorations withstood the T's blistering top speed of 45 miles per hour!

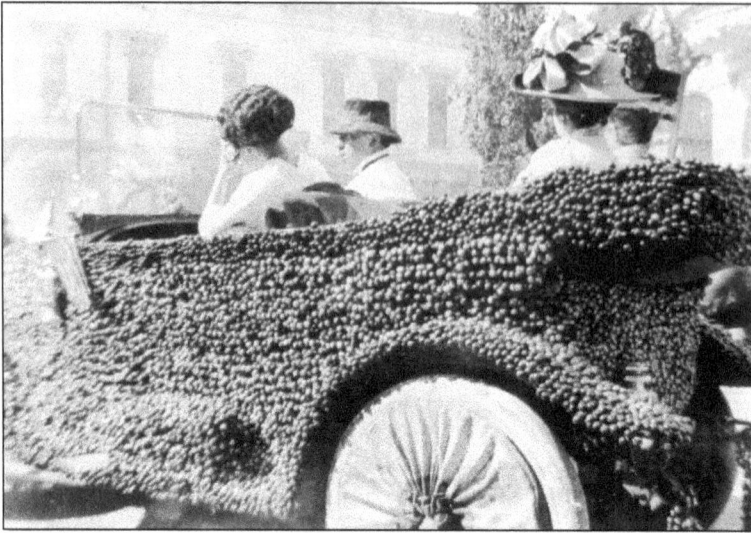

ANOTHER CAR FLOAT, C. 1910. These parade participants have painstakingly covered their auto with what appear to be cherries. Note the small American flag, perhaps an indication that the auto was used in Hayward's Fourth of July Parade. Also note the driver's position on the right side of this early automobile.

TOUR DE HAYWARD, 1900. Bicycle races were highly popular in the early 1900s. With competitions throughout the region, Hayward cyclists could load their mounts on the electric streetcars and arrive at the starting line fresh and ready to ride. Here Hayward cyclists race down Castro Street on the corner of A Street. The Haywards Livery Stable is clearly visible. The Eden Hotel is at the far end of the street.

PETERSEN GROCERY DELIVERY WAGON, 1910. Eugene Petersen crosses the horsecar tracks from the Southern Pacific depot up B Street. Peterson's Grocery was operated by two brothers and located on the corner of B and Main Streets.

FOURTH OF JULY PARADE, C. 1910. Getting in the Hayward spirit, the Petersens have brought out their buggy for the town's Fourth of July celebration. Such displays were a good opportunity for advertisement, as well as a chance to show individual patriotism. The Petersens clearly show their pride by decking out their horse in an Uncle Sam hat.

HAYWARD FAMILY PORTRAIT. The Sanholdt family—Kirsten, Johann, and their daughter, Emma—poses for the camera around 1900.

GROWING UP. Here Emma Sanholdt poses for her wedding portrait with groom, Henry Sorenson Sr. Emma designed the dress herself and sewed it by hand. The couple married in 1906.

OVER THERE. Hayward's Company H, 5th California Infantry Regiment, formed in 1909 out of a cadre of local veterans of the 1898 Spanish-American War. In 1916, during the civil upheaval in Mexico and following Pancho Villa's subsequent raids into New Mexico, Governor Hiram Johnson sent Company H to help protect residents of the Imperial Valley.

JESSE SILVA, C. 1918. Silva poses in a First World War–era U.S. Army uniform. Company H saw no action along the California-Mexico border. However, in April of 1917 the United States entered World War I and Hayward's youth were fighting in Europe. Four Hayward residents were awarded the Distinguished Service Cross; 12 lost their lives during the conflict.

RED CROSS PARADE, 1918. Members of the Hayward Grammar School band ride to a wartime parade in their Rosenberg Truck, while horse-drawn carriages share the streets with Model-T Fords.

HAYWARD TRAIN DEPOT, C. 1919. Relieved members of the Martin and Atkinson families wait for the troop train bringing a loved one home. This was the first, but certainly not the last, global war in which Hayward residents took part.

Five

Small Town in a Roaring Decade
1920–1930

With the end of the Great War, Hayward, like the rest of the nation, was anxious to return to what President Warren G. Harding termed "normalcy." However, the 1920s were anything but normal.

The early decade saw the destruction of the old Hayward's Hotel, and with the loss of the city's oldest landmark, one of Hayward's last physical ties to its role as a hostelry center was gone. Old traditions remained, however. Agriculture continued to be a mainstay of the city's economy, and the Hayward rodeo brought joy to thousands of fans throughout the years, harkening old residents back to the days of the Rancho San Lorenzo. The city's baseball teams played with the best the region could offer, and an important center of community life remained the city's schools.

But beyond the destruction of the old hotel, one of the greatest changes to Hayward was the increasing "automobility" of the town. Reveling in the prosperity of the times, increasing numbers of residents rejected the old streetcar line, trading in their trolley tickets for new Excelsior "auto cycles" and the Fords, Buicks, and Dodges now pouring out of America's factories. Auto dealers crowded the downtown, and the Hayward fire department proudly posed with its fleet of modern engines. With pedestrians and horses competing for space with increasing numbers of automobiles, perhaps no one represented the double-edged quality of California's burgeoning car culture more than Walter "Buck" Alves, the man hired as the city's first full-time traffic officer in 1923.

END OF AN ERA. Fire finally destroyed the old Hayward's Hotel in 1923. By the beginning of the 1920s most local hotels had deteriorated and the city lost its reputation as a rural resort. This photo was taken at the same angle as the earlier photo appearing on page 38.

BUT HAYWARD GOES ON. Here, cars crowd Hayward's downtown, probably the corner of B Street and Castro, around 1920. Parked on the right is a lonely looking horse-drawn buggy.

CITY GARAGE IN HAYWARD, 1920. By the 1920s, automobiles were a standard sight throughout Hayward, and 800 automobile enthusiasts came to town in 1922 before moving on to San Francisco to complete a transcontinental journey. The City Garage, owned by Clarence Manon, stood near A and First Streets and sold Ford and Buick automobiles.

DODGE BROTHER'S AUTO DEALERSHIP, C. 1920. If Fords and Buicks were not your cup of tea, you could purchase Dodge automobiles at the Walter H. Daniels dealership on the 200 block of Castro Street (Mission Boulevard). Beyond an expanding network of East Bay roads, by the end of the decade, Hayward car owners could take a Sunday drive across three new bridges: the San Mateo, the Dumbarton, and the Carquinez.

WALTER DANIELS. Here Daniels, president of Dodge Brothers Auto Dealer, test-drives a Dodge four-door Touring Sedan from the 1922–1927 era. The Dodge Brothers originally manufactured auto parts for other carmakers and were major investors in the Ford Motor Company. Using their profits, the brothers began their own automobile-manufacturing firm in 1914, granting franchises to dealers across the nation. Chrysler purchased the company in 1928.

GARAGE IN HAYWARD, 1921. Cars were much the rage in Hayward throughout the 1910s and 1920s. But like today, early automobiles spent a good part of the time at the repair shop.

HAYWARD TRAFFIC OFFICER. Faced with increasing congestion on city streets, in 1923 Walter J. "Buck" Alves became the city of Hayward's first full-time traffic officer. By the 1920s, California led the nation in new automobile registrations and, in part as a result of the new demand for gasoline, oil production. But traffic congestion was not the only social concern caused by the automobile. Increasing numbers of teenagers were in California high schools like Hayward's Union High, away from the supervision of their parents. More troublesome for self-appointed guardians of public decency was the changing design of the automobile. In 1919, roughly 90 percent of automobiles were open-topped. By 1927, over 80 percent of automobiles were enclosed. The resulting privacy within the vehicle caused one California police chief to lament that the greatest danger to the morality of youth was the coupe and the sedan.

PRIDE OF THE DEPARTMENT. Hayward's fire department poses for a group photo in front of its station on Castro Street sometime in the late 1920s. When this photo was taken, the community was planning to build its new city hall a block away. In the meantime, city meetings were held in the second story of the fire station. In the 1870s, Hayward was home to two volunteer fire companies: one on the corner of D and Atherton Streets, the other on Castro Street between B and C Streets. Like many volunteer fire companies at the time, the two companies utilized handcarts and buckets and competed with each to see who could respond and put down the fire first. By the time this photo was taken, the Hayward Fire Department was a dually staffed service with paid professionals supplemented by volunteers. The department became a fully-professional fire suppression and rescue service in the 1950s.

HAYWARD HIGH SCHOOL STUDENTS, 1924. This group of Hayward High seniors includes, from left to right, (front row) Frank Hahn, unidentified, Fred Foster, Doris Luce, Ruth Rathert, and Wilda Oswill; (back row) Gerald Hacket, Ellis Goforth, Irma Nelson, Muriel Christenson, Hazel Manter, Viola Jensen, Frances "Cappy" Ricks, and Abigail Quaas.

HAYWARD HIGH ATHLETES, 1924. Sitting, from left to right, are athletes Helen Alvez, an unidentified student, Katherine Rogers, Alberta Forth, Carol Diete, Margaret White, Irene Walters, unidentified, Florence Nicholson, unidentified, Alice Haley, Lillian O'Hanlon, and "Doughty."

MARKHAM SCHOOL DRUM CORPS. Here, seven members of the Markham Drum Corps pose before an event in this *c.* 1920 photo.

MARKHAM SCHOOL PHYSICAL EDUCATION, C. 1920. With more and more families trading physically demanding lives on the farm for relatively sedentary living in the city, increasing numbers of schools began to incorporate physical education classes into their curriculums. Note the dresses used as a standard exercise uniform.

HAYWARD HIGH SCHOOL BAND, 1925. As the 1925 Hayward High School annual declared, "the H.U.H.S. Band is a vital factor among the various High School organizations. In the past school year, the band has added zest to the Big Games of the year having turned out 100 percent strong at the Centerville football and the Richmond basketball games."

HAYWARD HIGH GIRLS GLEE CLUB, 1923. Pictured here, from left to right, are (front row) an unidentified student, Katherine Sweeney, Willette Burge, Elinor Thorndike, Deborah Nichols, Frances Winslow, Lola Kavanaugh, Lillian Martin, and Flossie Olivera; (back row) Elaine Reim, Edith Machado, unidentified, Isabel Diete, Ramona Hopkins, Gladys Browning, Elaine Glover, Ione Smyth, Thadea Rohn, Miriam Beauchamp, and Blanche Henningsen.

Hayward Grammar. Graduating CLass. JAN.22. 1926

HAYWARD GRAMMAR SCHOOL FACULTY AND STAFF. Teachers in small-town America were generally female, native-born, and in their mid-20s. In this 1922 photo of Hayward Grammar's faculty and staff, 43 of the 53 individuals are female.

HAYWARD GRAMMAR SCHOOL GRADUATING CLASS OF 1926. Seventy students posed for this class photo. The generation that emerged from Hayward Grammar during the 1920s would be faced with the challenges of the Great Depression.

HAYWARD LION'S CLUB. The Hayward Lion's Club poses with their mascot in this *c.* 1925 photo. Pictured here, from left to right, are (front row) Ed Friederichs, Ernie Blackman, Jim Willison, Jay Bruce, Hugh Linthicum, Wen Burke, Bill Hutchins, John Ravene, Peter Verzic, Chas Sorenson, George Meininger, G. Christiansen, and Bob Rhode; (back row) Tony Kelly, unidentified, Vince Strobel, Lloyd Russell, Hans Henningson, Raymond Bassett, Hans Ogard, two unidentified men, Carl Sorenson, Hal Angus, Ralph Reed, Herald Thorup, Frank Cunha, Walter Daniels, Rush Brunner, Bert Bedford, Nels Nelson, Wesley Armstrong, Leo Parry, and Robert Kruse. The Lions' occupations included a doctor, a dentist, a chiropractor, a banker, an electrician, a trucker, a barber, a butcher, a baker, a plumber, two competing car dealers, a radio dealer, grocers, a county employee, other business proprietors of various kinds, and a "state lion hunter."

ROTARY CLUB PICNIC. Originally called the "Barnacle Club" because of the shape of the ashtrays at their restaurant meeting place, the Hayward Rotary Club was formed in 1922 after convincing the regional headquarters that Hayward, with roughly 3,500 residents, was large enough to support its own chapter. Here Rotarians meet for a picnic.

HAYWARD ROTARIANS, C. 1920. The Rotary grew during the Roaring Twenties, largely because the subdivision of the 2,000-acre Meek Estate drew hundreds of new families to Hayward. The number of Rotarians declined during the Depression, but throughout the 1930s the Hayward Rotary continued to support the local Boy Scouts, and at Christmas, they sponsored a movie matinee and party for underprivileged children. Here Rotarians apparently make light of Prohibition.

HAYWARD 20/30 CLUB FLOAT. The Hayward 20/30 Club was a popular men's organization throughout the 1920s. During the Depression the group joined the Hayward Rotary and Lions Clubs to hold an annual Halloween party for local children at the Hayward Plunge. Here the club takes part in a 1927 parade with their float, a replica of Charles Lindbergh's *Spirit of St. Louis*.

HAYWARD 20/30 CLUB PARTY. The 20/30 Club, like Hayward's other fraternal groups, sponsored various events for the community's underprivileged children. Here the 20/30ers host their annual Christmas party on December 19, 1929.

CHILDREN'S PARADE, C. 1920. Here, local schoolchildren, probably from the Markham School, parade down B Street.

HAYWARD ENTRY, OAKLAND PARADE, 1924. Hayward citizens also participated in the celebrations of neighboring communities. Here, the Hayward entry in Oakland's Dons of Peralta Parade strikes an attractive pose. By 1920, Oakland's population was over 216,261, making Hayward, with slightly over 3,500 residents, a small but charming town. By comparison, San Francisco's 1920 population was 576,676.

BASEBALL IN HAYWARD. Various Hayward organizations, from the Native Sons of the Golden West to the American Legion, sponsored baseball teams to compete in local leagues. Here Madsen's Variety team, representing a local grocer on B Street, poses for the camera in 1925. Although Major League Baseball prohibited African Americans from playing until 1948, Madsen's team appears ahead of their time.

HAYWARD MERCHANTS BASEBALL TEAM, 1929. Local merchants also formed a competitive team. Pictured here, from left to right, are (front row) Mel Travers, Al Cambria, Fil Soares, Dutch Rottiger, and Migg Rogerson; (back row) team manager John Mitchel, Charlie Jensen, Al Swape, George Forth, Clayton Whited (known as "Lefty"), Buck Grendell, Tony Alameda, and coach Joe Riggs.

HAYWARD EASY RIDER, 1920. In this photo, Jamie and Louie Stricker appear atop their newfangled transport. The Excelsior auto cycle they are riding was an early version of the modern motorcycle.

EASY RIDER AND PASSENGER, 1920. With a two-cylinder engine and a single gear, the right-hand grip of the Excelsior controlled the throttle and the left-hand grip controlled the clutch. This was the first motorcycle to have such an arrangement. This time Louie poses on his motorbike with Mary Stricker, apparently riding sidesaddle.

THE HAYWARD RODEO, 1926. Harry Rowell began organizing rodeos in Hayward in the 1920s on his ranch on Mattox Road. In 1921, he and his wife, Maggie, held annual two-day competitions on the grounds of Bret Harte School. Because of its popularity, in 1929 Rowell moved the rodeo to his ranch in Dublin Canyon. The annual event harkened Hayward residents back to the days of the Rancho San Lorenzo Alta.

ROWELL RANCH, c. 1930. Rowell provided the livestock for the Hayward rodeo, leasing the animals out to cowboys for the competition. In 1932, Rowell purchased 1,000 Mexican horses. The mustangs were selected to participate in the rodeo; the others went straight to the pet food factory. Here is an aerial photo of the ranch, c. 1930.

CAR FLOAT. This Hayward auto was the winning float in the 1927 Farm Product Show. Driving is Mrs. Macabe. In the front passenger seat is Mrs. Kavanagh. Riding in the back, from left to right, are Mable Jaimerson, Mrs. King, and Mrs. Brown.

HAYWARD WEDDING STYLES. Mabel Rhode Willits and Harvey Willits pose for their wedding picture in front of Dania Hall in April 1928.

PICKING FRUIT IN HAYWARD. As central Hayward continued to urbanize, agriculture remained an important part of the regional economy. By 1925, the annual income derived from the truck crops, deciduous fruit, and poultry of old Eden Township, of which Hayward was part, was estimated at $3 million. In that same year, Hayward farmers dedicated 600 acres to cherries, 800 acres to pears, and 1,500 acres to tomatoes.

HAYWARD POULTRY PRODUCERS. Hayward was also home to numerous poultry farms. By 1919, Alameda County placed sixth in the state in the total number of fowl, and by the mid-1920s the county bird population was estimated at 1.2 million. Hayward Poultry Producers was formed in 1908 as a cooperative association of the city's poultry farmers. The HPP sold farm supplies, including feed, at cost to its 900 members.

HUNT'S DOCKWORKERS. Here dockworkers handle an assortment of Hunt's products at the Hayward plant. By the 1920s, Hunt's employed 400 to 1,000 people, depending on the season. They canned spinach in March, cherries in May, apricots in June, and peaches in July. Employees also processed tomatoes during the summer, which were then canned or made into catsup, puree, and hot sauce.

TAKING A BREAK AT HUNT'S. Seasonal cannery work was difficult, but in the 1920s Hunt's provided a number of amenities for its workforce, including a modern cafeteria equipped to simultaneously feed 1,000 employees during the peak season. The plant also incorporated a first-aid station, as well as a small cluster of worker housing. Here, cannery workers, the majority of them women, enjoy their break.

RODERICK'S FRUIT DRYER. Operated by Manuel Roderick and Mary (Silva) Roderick, Roderick's Fruit Dryer on Orchard Avenue dried apricots and pears for market. Beyond is the future site of Alameda State College, now California State University, Hayward.

RODERICK'S DRYER INTERIOR. Hayward was a center of the fruit-drying industry in the first decades of the 20th century. Here Roderick's Dryer employees tend to their duties.

MOUNTAINS OF SALT. Mount Eden has been a center of the salt industry since the 1850s, when John Johnson harvested a 25-ton salt crop from pools north of the present location of the San Mateo Bridge. Seventeen family-based salt-producing concerns were operating between San Lorenzo and Alameda Creeks by the late 1860s.

MORTON SALT PLANT. East Bay salt production remained strong in the 20th century. Much of Hayward's salt was destined for the Morton refining plant in nearby Newark. In 1910, the company developed a salt that would be free-running in damp weather, as well as a moisture-proof package. To highlight their innovations, the company chose as their symbol a little girl with an umbrella, easily pouring salt in the rain.

Six

CHALLENGE AND
EXPANSION
1930–1940

October 1929 saw the stock market crash and America was plunged into the Great Depression. Unemployment in California's largest cities skyrocketed to 25 percent, farm income was cut in half, and roughly one-fifth of state residents survived by accepting some form of public relief. Over one million refugees from the Dust Bowl came to California, lured by the promise of work and sun. By 1940, these real-life versions of Steinbeck's Joad family made up one-seventh of California's population, yet many residents viewed them as an intolerable drain on the state's already overstretched resources.

Hayward was not immune to the challenges of the Depression. When a number of downtown businesses closed, farmers found the unemployed waiting to be hired as pickers during harvest time, and migrants from the Midwest took work usually reserved for locals at the packing plants.

In spite of the hardships, the 1930s was also a time of expansion for the city of Hayward. The construction of a new city hall and veteran's memorial building added to the city's civic architecture during the early years of the economic crisis. Later, New Deal funds built such landmarks as the Hayward Plunge, the Hayward Water Tower on Hesperian Avenue, and the Bret Harte School. Local business owners donated food to local relief kitchens. The community's Lions, Rotary, and 20/30 Clubs sponsored swimming contests and pet parades. With war clouds on the horizon, Hayward was battered, but the community shined.

BIRD'S-EYE VIEW OF HAYWARD, C. 1935. Much of downtown Hayward is visible in this early aerial photo. During the Depression, a number of Hayward's most recognizable structures were built, including the downtown post office, old city hall, the veterans memorial building, the Hesperian Water Tower, and the Hayward Plunge. Foothill Boulevard and Jackson Street were joined as part of a series of street improvements that also benefited the town. In the photo above, looking towards the northeast, Hayward City Hall is visible in the lower right corner. To the right of city hall are the steeple-topped Native Sons Hall and the Markham School. Densely built B Street is at the center of the photo, and the white cluster of buildings at the top is Hayward's Union High School. The area around Union High is now the site of the Civic Center Plaza.

HAYWARD STREET SCENE, C. 1940. This photo looks southeast from the corner of Main and B Streets. In spite of the apparent bustle, downtown Hayward, like the rest of California, felt the pains of the Great Depression and a number of businesses closed.

CAN I BORROW THE CAR? A group of Hayward Union High School students cram into a rather worn crank-start automobile in the late 1930s.

Hayward Street Scene, 1930s. In this photo, looking east on B Street, a nanny walks her charge across Castro Street (now Mission Boulevard), *c.* 1938. The Schafer building, the white structure in the foreground, housed a number of retail shops until fire destroyed it in 1987.

Hayward Street Scene, c. 1940. By the end of the 1930s, Hayward's economy was showing signs of recovery, a fact underscored by the heavy traffic on the corner of Main and B Streets.

AGRICULTURAL EMPLOYEES, C. 1935. The Depression also had an impact on Hayward's agriculture. Many Hayward residents used seasonal work at the town's packing and drying plants to help make ends meet. The appearance of competitors from the Midwest, their own region devastated by the Dust Bowl, dashed their hopes. In spite of the hardships, this diverse group of employees at Gus King's Fruit Dryer appears confident in the future.

HAYWARD KEEPS WORKING. These Hayward workers, possibly employed by the WPA, complete a job on the grounds surrounding the Hayward Plunge. Many Depression-era Californians depended on New Deal public works programs like the Public Works Administration, the Works Progress Administration, and the Civilian Conservation Corps for employment.

CITY HALL UNDER CONSTRUCTION, 1931. In 1930, Hayward constructed its first permanent city hall on Castro Street, a $100,000 structure that concentrated all city departments in a single location. The cornerstone of the new hall was laid on May 17, 1930. Superintendent of construction Leroy Lawrence experienced the first bad omen when his work crews had to dig 12 feet deeper than anticipated to lay the foundation for the building's front steps. Finding only loose rock, the lack of a sound surface for the hall's foundation was blamed on the Hayward Fault. Nevertheless, construction of Hayward's new city hall was completed the following year. In 1989, the Loma Prieta earthquake seriously damaged the interior of the building and forced its closure. Thanks to the efforts of groups like the Friends of City Hall, a compromise was reached whereby the building's shell would be preserved, but the interior will probably never be repaired. Although predating the New Deal's public works projects, construction of the hall in the early 1930s provided much-needed jobs during hard times.

HAYWARD CITY HALL, C. 1940. Hayward's 1930s-era city hall served as the center of local government for 30 years until fault creep warranted its closure. Municipal offices moved to the civic center in the 1970s, until that, too, was declared seismically unsafe. Finally, Hayward government moved to its new award-winning city hall, dedicated in January 1999, complete with base isolators that allow the building to move with the ground.

VETERANS MEMORIAL BUILDING. Built on Main Street, the veterans memorial building opened in January 1932 and housed the Hayward chapter of the USO during World War II . In 2000, the County of Alameda rededicated the building as the Allen F. Strutz Veterans Memorial Building to honor a lifelong advocate for Bay Area veterans. The two siege guns displayed at the building's entrance were captured during World War I.

109

OPENING DAY OF THE HAYWARD PLUNGE. Funded by a $69,000 bond and a $26,000 grant from the New Deal's Works Progress Administration, the Hayward Plunge opened in 1936 in Memorial Park. Beyond recreation, the project provided much-needed employment for local construction crews.

CROWD ENJOYING THE PLUNGE, C. 1936. Sunbathers enjoy the outer concourse of the Plunge after taking advantage of the indoor pool. Today, Hayward swimmers and sunbathers still enjoy the Plunge, operated by the Hayward Area Recreation and Park District.

HAYWARD SWIMMERS, C. 1939. Here four Hayward girls enjoy the Plunge. With an alteration of hairstyle and swimming fashion, the photo could have been taken in 2004. Among the swimmers are Margery Roberts, Marilyn Strobridge, and Margery Poole.

NRA Construction Crew. An important component of F.D.R.'s early New Deal was the National Recovery Administration, which included among its duties, oversight of various public works projects. Here an NRA crew works on the new Hayward water tower on Hesperian Boulevard. Worker Manuel J. Moniz stands at left.

Hayward Water Tower. The tower nears completion. Today the Hayward water tower is visible to thousands of Bay Area commuters on Interstate 880.

HAYWARD PARADE FLOAT, C. 1935. Hayward's growth definitely slowed during the Depression. Between 1920 and 1930, thanks to a booming national economy and the increasing subdivision and sale of area farmland, Hayward's population increased by over 2,000 people, from 3,487 to 5,530. However, during the 1930s the city's rate of growth slowed. By 1940, the city's population stood at 6,736, an increase of only 1,206. During the 1920s, the vast majority of new city residents were homeseekers, but during the Depression, many new arrivals were impoverished migrants searching for work. Hayward relied on tried and true methods to recapture its former prosperity and growth. One means was to participate in out-of-town celebrations, hoping to lure new residents by highlighting the advantages of moving to the community. This local float, probably participating in a parade in San Francisco, advertises Hayward's rural charm.

AMERICAN LEGION POST NO. 68. Hayward's American Legion band poses during the 1930s. Former members of the American Expeditionary Force that fought in France during World War I formed the Legion in 1919. By 1931, the Legion counted over one million veterans as members, including these Hayward Legionnaires. The band of Post Number 68 played at numerous events during the 1930s. The continued prominence of Hayward's civic organizations helped create a sense of normalcy during hard times. Members include, from left to right, (front row) William Silva, J.W. Sherwood, Leo Hogreff, Frank Erickson, Director Leo Hillings, E.D. McDonald, Clarence E. Johnson, Cecil Jodkins, and W.M. Howell; (second row) Edgar Riley, Ed Call, Henry Ecuyer, Fred Wallace, Charles Sorenson, and two unidentified members; (third row) Frank Soares, C.F. Andrade, Bruce Vicar, Edgar Hizer, unidentified, and Joseph Holingshead; (fourth row) P.E. Homan, Eugene McBarron, Inol Blamgria, Robert Ruife, Gus Boremen, George Lewis, and Art Phillips.

114

NATIVE DAUGHTERS OF THE GOLDEN WEST, 1940. Women's groups likewise maintained their sense of community activism. Here the Native Daughters pose during a social occasion.

WHERE EVERYBODY KNOWS YOUR NAME. During a period when most Hayward residents needed a stiff drink, they could—thanks to the end of Prohibition—get it at places like Danny's Cocktail Lounge in San Lorenzo Village, which provided much-needed relaxation. The presence of the serviceman at left indicates that the photo was probably taken around 1940.

BASEBALL. Hayward continued to be a center of East Bay baseball throughout the Depression. Here, the Hayward Merchant's Baseball Team poses with their diminutive mascot at San Leandro Park in 1934.

BASEBALL. Some Hayward businesses deflected the pressures of declining sales by continuing their tradition of fielding company baseball teams. The Donner-Herbert Ford baseball team poses for the camera at Hayward Union High School, *c.* 1940.

PET PARADE. By the 1930s, the Lion's Club sponsored an annual pet parade, adding to Hayward's list of annual celebrations and beginning a tradition that drew increasing numbers of participants and spectators throughout the 1940s and 1950s. The parade route took marchers from the Markham School down B Street. Participants were awarded with ice cream or candy. Here, Vernon Gabel shows off his prize-winning goat, c. 1938.

PET PARADE, C. 1940. By the 1940s, the East Bay was home to a growing community of Japanese immigrants. Here Japanese-American schoolchildren from the John Muir School show off a float created for participation in an annual pet parade.

PET PARADE, C. 1940. This photo shows another view of Japanese-American schoolchildren participating in the Hayward Pet Parade, *c.* 1940.

MOUNT EDEN JAPANESE SCHOOL, C. 1940. Japanese-American schoolchildren from the Mount Eden Japanese School pose with their teacher, Mrs. Sakakura. Pictured, from left to right, are Mineko Nakomura, Masake Sagino, Hisaye Tomatoshi, Chiyoko Fujino, Miyeko Akagi, Yasako Ichikawa, Yoshika Negi, Fusage Obata, Hamoko Hamasaki, two unidentified children, Yoshiye Yada, Kiyoko Matsai, Sumiko Matsai, Yakiko Yada, and Kikuye Tomatoshi.

HAYWARD THEATER, C. 1940. The Bay Area had been one of the cradles of the early motion-picture industry. Just to the south of Hayward, in Niles Canyon, Essanay Studios produced 375 Bronco Billy westerns between 1910 and 1916, and Charlie Chaplin filmed his most famous film, *The Tramp*. By 1920, the industry was located almost exclusively in Southern California, but Hayward movie attendance climbed. Although the advent of the talkies in the late 1920s increased movie attendance, during the early years of the Great Depression the industry suffered from declining ticket sales and a rash of theater closures across the nation. By the late 1930s, Hollywood had recovered from the Depression and entered its Golden Age, producing 400 feature-length films annually for a weekly audience of 80 million. Here, a crowd lines up at the Hayward Theater to view Tony Martin in *Casbah*. Elenore Thorndike is the overworked ticket-taker.

BRIDGE CLUB, C. 1940. If you were not a movie fan, you could always join the Hayward Bridge Club. Pictured, from left to right, are Aurora Macabee, Irene O'Connor, Gladys Luce, Margaret Manter, Irene Halley, Cora Simpson, Josephine Cone Peferlee, and Susie Klee.

END OF THE STREETCAR. By 1940, members of the Hayward Bridge Club would no longer take the trolley to their tournaments. In the early 1930s, the Key System acquired the passenger bus franchise rights from Peerless Stage Lines in South Alameda County. In 1934, the system ended the Hayward to Oakland streetcar run. The era of the passenger bus began, augmented with the establishment of BART in 1972.

CITY FIRE FIGHTERS IN FRONT OF THE HAYWARD POST OFFICE. Hayward firefighters pose with their engines in front of the Hayward post office, *c.* 1940. In 1915, under Fire Chief Manuel Riggs, the Hayward Fire Department retired its horses and acquired its first fire truck. The first engine driver was John Carr, who had never driven a motor vehicle before his appointment. By the time this photo was taken in front of what was then the new Hayward Post Office, the department had a number of engines. The post office, built in 1938, began as a local project and was completed under the auspices of the Works Progress Administration, one of F.D.R.'s New Deal public works programs. True to the WPA's function, construction of the post office provided desperately needed jobs.

BRET HARTE SCHOOL. Another New Deal public works project in 1938 combined city and WPA funds for the construction of Bret Harte Junior High School. The school is located on E Street, near downtown.

STUDENT ACTIVISM IN THE DEPRESSION ERA. Protests weren't just reserved for the 1960s. Here Hayward Union High students conduct a 1937 "strike" in support of fired Vice Principal H.S. Hampton, who was eventually rehired.

OTTO EMERSON. For 40 years Otto Emerson, "Hayward's Artist and Naturalist," wrote pieces for ornithological publications, expanded the U.S. government's list of bird species, set out on several ornithological expeditions, and was an expert on the migratory patterns of birds in the Hayward area. By the 1930s, Emerson was in his 70s, but that did not prevent him from serving as a teacher and scout examiner for the Alameda Boy Scouts.

OTTO EMERSON PICKING DAFFODILS. By the 1930s, over two million daffodils bloomed at Emerson's Palm Cottage home. Each spring Emerson picked daffodils, loaded them onto a wooden cart and, in spite of a malformed hip, pushed them downtown to sell. Uninterested in the money, Emerson simply wanted to share the beauty with his fellow citizens. Hayward residents gave Emerson the title, "Daffodil King."

SHELL STATION. In spite of hard times, Hayward's autos kept rolling, but not fast enough for Walt Alpers's Shell Station in the village of San Lorenzo.

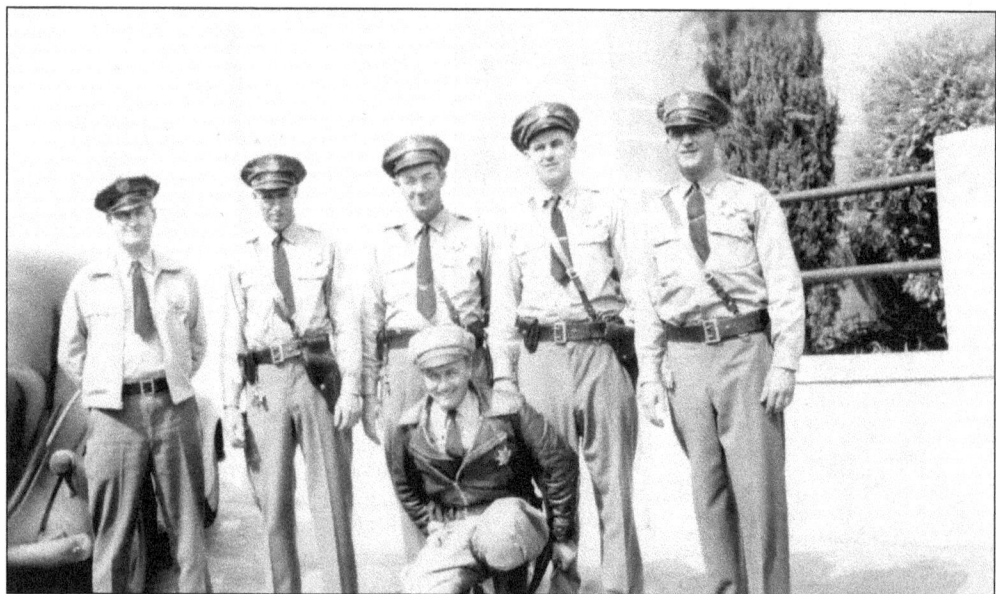

HAYWARD POLICE. The Hayward Police Department experienced its first death of an officer in the line of duty when patrolman George Vierria was shot in 1929 during a domestic disturbance at 1261 B Street. The mid-1930s were happier times for the department. Posing here, from left to right, are officers Forth, Burge, Patterson, Hinch, Harrier, and Marchand.

Friendly Handshake. Here California Highway Patrol captain L.A. Eike greets a local citizen at the Oliver Deshow Mobile Station on B Street. The state legislature created the California Highway Patrol on August 14, 1929, to enforce traffic laws on county and state highways. Besides automobiles, the CHP has also used motorcycles as patrol vehicles since its inception. Captain Eike's cruiser is a 1932 Ford with a "flathead" V-8 engine. With 25 more horsepower than a standard Model A, the vehicle was a natural choice for the Depression-era CHP. When Eike patrolled the East Bay, the region's modern highway system was not yet in place. Foothill Boulevard formed part of U.S. Highway 50 and was the primary route to Oakland; Hesperian and Castro (now Mission) were the main routes to San Jose; Livermore was reached using the Dublin Road.

NEWS STAND, C. 1940. A local newspaper dealer smiles for the camera, but ominous headlines announce the sinking of neutral ships by German U-Boats.

FIELD TRIP, C. 1940. With America in economic crisis and the world moving towards war, Hayward institutions tried to maintain a sense of stability and continuity. Here, Markham School students take a field trip to Mission San Jose. Many local schoolchildren can recall a class outing to Mission San Jose or completing the perennial fourth-grade project of building a model of a mission complex. Such activities keep alive an important link to Hayward's past.

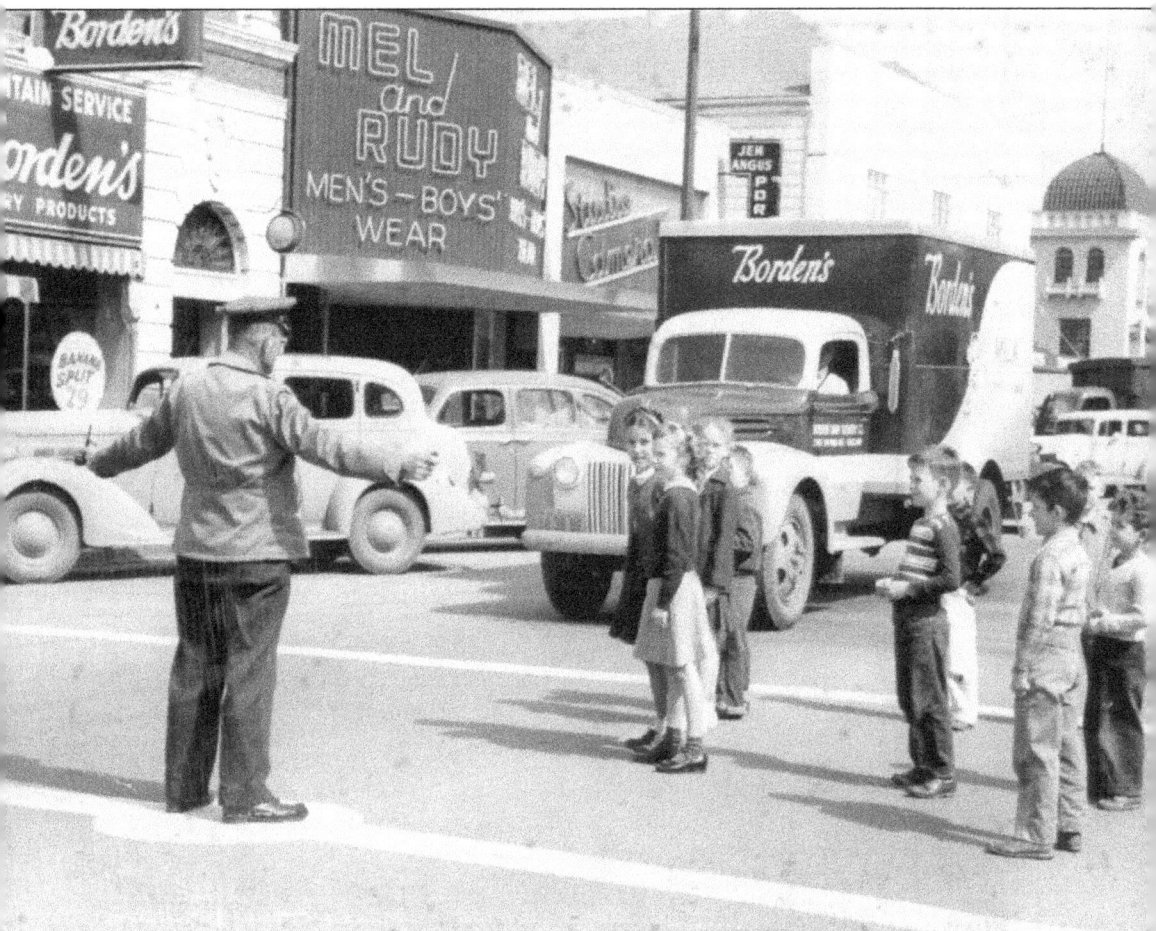

SAFE AT HOME. With war approaching, it was safe to be home. Markham School students cross B Street, protected by traffic guard Lewis Hansen. Their destination is unknown, but a good guess would be the Borden Dairy Shop, where kids could enjoy 29¢ banana splits. A Borden's supply truck waits for the potential customers to cross. Behind the truck is the Hayward (Carnegie) Library. Buffalo Bill's brewery and restaurant now occupies part of the block in the immediate background.

CROSSING INTO A NEW ERA. Throughout the early part of the century, a narrow swinging bridge crossed San Lorenzo Creek, connecting Hayward High School to Russell Way. The peninsula, formed by the creek and a small tributary, was known as Botany Grounds, an area that was incorporated into Hayward High's campus grounds in the 1930s. Here, a Hayward resident negotiates the rickety bridge. Soon the United States would be drawn into the World War II, and Hayward would be changed forever.

Visit us at
arcadiapublishing.com

www.ingramcontent.com/pod-product-compliance
Lightning Source LLC
Chambersburg PA
CBHW080623110426
42813CB00006B/1588